Object-Oriented Programming in ColdFusion

Break free from procedural programming and learn how to optimize your applications and enhance your skills using objects and design patterns

Matt Gifford

PUBLISHING

BIRMINGHAM - MUMBAI

Object-Oriented Programming in ColdFusion

First published: October 2010

Production Reference: 1081010

Published by Packt Publishing Ltd.
32 Lincoln Road
Olton
Birmingham, B27 6PA, UK.

ISBN 978-1-847196-32-3

www.packtpub.com

Cover Image by Filippo (filosarti@tiscali.it)

Credits

Author
Matt Gifford

Reviewer
Raymond Camden

Acquisition Editor
David Barnes

Development Editor
Dhiraj Chandiramani

Rakesh Shejwal

Technical Editor
Arun Nadar

Copy Editor
Laxmi Subramanian

Indexer
Rekha Nair

Editorial Team Leader
Aditya Belpathak

Project Team Leader
Priya Mukherji

Project Coordinator
Leena Purkait

Proofreader
Lynda Sliwoski

Production Coordinator
Alwin Roy

Cover Work
Alwin Roy

Foreword

ColdFusion Components (or CFCs) were introduced in ColdFusion MX back in 2002, and since then they have become one of the most important and fundamental building blocks for ColdFusion developers. In fact, recent releases of ColdFusion have made CFC use mandatory, by introducing features that are only available through ColdFusion Components.

As you'd expect from ColdFusion, CFCs are easy to learn and even easier to use. But the beautiful simplicity of ColdFusion Components hides a powerful, sophisticated, and proven Java-based framework on which developers can build highly scalable and manageable applications. Like all ColdFusion features, CFCs can be as simple or as sophisticated as your application requires, and developers can start reaping their benefits easily and painlessly, adding functionality and complexity later as needed.

But this duel personality, highly accessible simplicity on the one hand and all that power on the other, has proven to be a bit of a double-edged sword. The same ease of use that makes ColdFusion so easy to learn and so productive, also makes it too easy to never fully explore and leverage all that ColdFusion has to offer.

This is why I am so glad to see Matt Gifford's hard work take the form of this book. Matt starts with the basics of ColdFusion Components, but then quickly delves into the subtleties and complexities of using them for object-oriented development, demonstrating both the how's and why's, as well as the tips and tricks needed to truly appreciate how ColdFusion Components can (and should) change the way you build your next ColdFusion application.

Matt, this book is long overdue, and your contribution to the ColdFusion community is greatly appreciated. Thanks!

Ben Forta

Director of Platform Evangelism

Adobe Systems

When you start using ColdFusion components, you know that you're on the right track; you can feel this change at some core, instinctual level—as if you're about to embrace something that holds tremendous, yet untapped potential. Unfortunately, your instincts won't take you much further beyond this point. The cold reality is, Object-Oriented Programming (OOP), when used incorrectly, is a destructive force that can leave your code tightly coupled, brittle, and nearly impossible to maintain.

And yet, wave after wave of graduating computer scientists come to hail OOP as the only way to build robust and durable software. Now, this is not proof of a poor educational system; rather, it is a testament to the tried and true benefits of an object-oriented approach to software development. This commitment to OOP reinforces those instinctual feelings we experience as we type out the code "CFComponent"—we are on the right path to good development practice.

With great power comes great responsibility, and Object-Oriented Programming is a powerful tool. By reading this book and choosing to further your understanding of OOP, you are demonstrating great responsibility! Learning OOP the right way is the only responsible choice that you can make for yourself and for your clients.

Ben Nadel

Chief Software Engineer

Epicenter Consulting

To go Object-Oriented or to not go Object-Oriented (OO) is still the source of some of the most heated discussions in the ColdFusion world. The simple truth is that the rest of the programming world had this fight 10 years ago—and OO won. As a result of the wider industry's move towards OO, the ColdFusion community has also embraced this methodology; this has been done by adapting frameworks and patterns from other languages. The product teams at Adobe have adopted OO by introducing ColdFusion Components and Object Relational Mapping to the list of features within and available to ColdFusion.

Where does that leave the average ColdFusion developer, those people who don't have time to learn every new tag and function added to ColdFusion with each release? They're too busy working for a living, which makes finding the time and resources for ongoing professional development a real challenge.

Often it leaves these ColdFusion developers with no starting point, no easy onramp, to "get their OO on". This is a shame, and somewhat of an irony, as OO can be a highway to productivity. However, without a guide, exploring OO can be like travelling down a forested dirt road in the middle of the night. You can easily go off track.

That's why I was thrilled to hear that Matt Gifford had agreed to write the book you have in your hands. Matt is one of those hard to find technical minds that can communicate as well as he codes. I can think of no one better to help you navigate the sometimes tough, but always rewarding road that is Object-Oriented programming.

Terry Ryan

ColdFusion Evangelist

Adobe Systems

About the Author

Matt Gifford like many developers began his career teaching himself the basics of software development. Starting with simple applications using BASIC Programming on his Sinclair ZX Spectrum, he moved to creating relational databases in VBScript and hand-coding HTML pages in text editors. From at-home 'hobby' programming, Matt moved into the world of professional development in 2000 before getting a role as a web developer with the UNEP, where he was trained in ColdFusion. Matt later moved to agency and contract roles in London, where he also picked up new languages including Adobe Flex and AIR.

Now as a Lead Developer with Fuzzy Orange Ltd, Matt continues to specialize in ColdFusion, Flex, and AIR development. He presents regularly at national and international conferences and online meetings, and has written tutorials and articles for online resources and leading UK industry magazines.

As an Adobe Community Professional for ColdFusion, Matt is a keen proponent for community resources and sharing knowledge. He regularly writes and releases open source ColdFusion applications and code samples, which he shares through his blog, www.mattgifford.co.uk, as well as supporting the community online in forums and social media.

Acknowledgement

No publication or piece of work is ever the product of one individual, and these are just some of the people I need to thank.

Thank you to Douglas Paterson, Leena Purkait, and the Packt Publishing team who have helped guide me through all the challenges of writing my first book.

I would like to thank Ray Camden and Ben Nadel for technically reviewing this publication in various states and for providing suggestions and ideas from day one of this project.

Massive thanks goes out to John Whish, who shared his time so that we could discuss paradigms, patterns, and the intricacies of using cars as code examples.

Of course, thank you to the ColdFusion product team and to Adobe, for continuing to improve an already amazing product, and to the entire ColdFusion community, which justly deserves the reputation as being a supportive and committed group of professionals.

Finally, thank you to my amazing wife Cate who has supported me throughout this process, with patience, advice, and encouragement.

About the Reviewer

Raymond Camden is a software consultant focusing on ColdFusion and RIA development. A long time ColdFusion user, Raymond has worked on numerous ColdFusion books including the ColdFusion Web Application Construction Kit and has contributed to the Fusion Authority Quarterly Update and the ColdFusion Developers Journal. He also presents at conferences and contributes to online webzines. He founded many community websites including CFLib.org, ColdFusionPortal.org, and ColdFusionCookbook.org and is the author of open source applications, including the popular BlogCFC (www.blogcfc.com) blogging application. Raymond can be reached at his blog (www.coldfusionjedi.com) or through e-mail at ray@camdenfamily.com. He is the happily married proud father of three kids and is somewhat of a Star Wars nut.

Table of Contents

Preface   **1**

Chapter 1: Introducing ColdFusion Components   **7**

Why use CFCs?   **8**
Grouping your functions   9
Organizing your components   9
The ColdFusion component tags   **10**
Our first component   **10**
Defining a method   11
Returning the data   11
ColdFusion 9 scripted components   12
Creating your object   12
Restricting your functions to scopes   **13**
Using arguments within your methods   14
The Arguments scope   14
Redefine the function parameters   15
Combining your methods   16
Protecting your local variables   **17**
Using the Var scope   20
Placing your Var scoped variables   21
Naming your Var scoped variables   21
Accessing your CFC   **22**
Instantiating the object   22
Using the createObject function   22
Using the cfobject tag   23
Using the NEW operator   23
Using cfinvoke   23
The cfinvoke tag   24
Using cfinvokeargument   24
Using attributes as arguments   24
Using an argument collection   25

Passing arguments into an instance method call   **25**

As a list   25

As named values   26

As an argumentCollection   26

Arguments in action   **26**

Merging your functions into one   26

Using cfargument to combine your methods   27

Creating an object constructor   **29**

Creating an init() function   30

The Variables scope   31

Calling your init() function   32

The This scope   32

Summary   **35**

Chapter 2: Effective Component Development   **37**

Pseudo-constructors   **37**

Using the pseudo method   38

Suppressing whitespace   39

Output attribute   40

Pseudo-constructor or init() method   41

Returning values and variables   **42**

returnType   42

Access properties   **45**

Private   46

Package   47

Public   47

Remote   47

Getting information about your CFC   **47**

Introspection   48

CFC Explorer   48

Component Doc   49

Document your code   50

Benefits of documentation   50

Displayname attribute   50

Hint attribute   50

Description attribute   51

User-defined metadata   51

Obtaining CFC metadata   52

getMetaData   52

getComponentMetaData   54

Returning metadata   55

Detailed introspection   **56**

Summary   **57**

Chapter 3: Building Your First Bean   **59**
What is a Bean?   **59**
But what is it really?   60
The benefit of using beans   **62**
Creating our first Bean   **63**
An introduction to UML   63
Person object in UML   64
What makes a Bean a Bean   66
A default/no-argument constructor   66
Easily accessible for introspection   67
Completing our Projects Bean   68
Calling our project Bean   72
Populating the Bean   **73**
Read/Write Bean   74
Read-only Bean   76
Helpful objects   **77**
Implicit accessors   **82**
Summary   **86**

Chapter 4: Inheritance and Object-Oriented Concepts   **87**
What is Inheritance?   **87**
Avoiding code duplication   90
Inheriting our products   91
The Super keyword   95
Overriding methods   95
Instantiating our products   96
The inheritance hierarchy   **98**
Specialization   98
The "IS A" relationship   99
Polymorphism   **99**
Composition   **100**
The "HAS A" Relationship   100
Implied ownership   103
Aggregation   **103**
Summary   **109**

Chapter 5: Data Access Objects   **111**
What is a Data Access Object?   **111**
Creating a Data Access Object   **112**
The create method   116
Storing a new user   118
The read method   121
Handling select results   122
The update method   123

The delete method   128
An alternative save method   129
The save method   129
The exists method   130
Caching the Data Access Objects   132
Dependency Injection   **133**
Summary   **134**
Chapter 6: Gateways   **135**
What is a Gateway?   **136**
A typical ColdFusion Gateway   **136**
Creating a Gateway object   138
Naming conventions   138
Adding gateway methods   140
Minimising code duplication   143
Revising the gateway object   144
Caching the Gateway object   147
The Gateway discussion   **148**
No hard and fast rules   148
Table Data Gateway   148
Similarities to Data Access Objects   149
Combining the two patterns   150
Which option is best?   151
Summary   **152**
Chapter 7: Creating a Service Layer   **153**
What is a Service Layer?   **154**
Facade patterns in a nutshell   155
Creating a service   **155**
Defining the User Service   157
Adding the CRUD methods   158
Adding the Gateway methods   160
Adding an abstract class   162
Defining the address service   **163**
onApplicationStart (revisited)   166
Summary   **167**
Index   **169**

Preface

The principles and fundamental elements of Object-Oriented Programming (OOP) are not new to the development world, although for some, there is a hesitancy to engage with OOP as it can be perceived as a confusing or unnecessary method of development.

As you read *Object-Oriented Programming in ColdFusion*, you will be guided through the core structure of ColdFusion Components, the foundation of OOP in CFML-based applications, and an introduction to some common design patterns and principles used in object-oriented development.

This book deals with the basic fundamental practices of OOP, including object creation and reuse, Bean objects, service layers, Data Access Objects, and simple design patterns. This is intended to help the reader gain a better understanding of OOP using examples that can be altered and applied into any application.

Object-Oriented Programming in ColdFusion aims to simplify the understanding of OOP, and dispense with unnecessary jargon and complex diagrams. By taking this more direct approach, this book aims to assist the reader in understanding the principles of OOP, how to implement them into their ColdFusion applications, and help the user extend their development skills in the process.

Using the practical examples within this easy-to-follow guide, you will learn how to structure your applications and code, and apply the fundamental basics of OOP to develop modular and reusable components that will scale easily with your application. This is ideal for any ColdFusion developer looking to break free from writing purely procedural code, and extend and advance their development practices.

Who this book is for

If you are a web developer wanting to implement object-oriented programming with ColdFusion, then this book is for you. If your goal is to get a good grounding in the basics of the object-oriented programming concepts, this book is perfect for you. No prior knowledge of object-oriented programming is expected, but basic knowledge of ColdFusion development run skills is assumed.

What this book covers

Chapter 1, Introducing ColdFusion Components outlines the basic elements of ColdFusion Components. The reader is guided through the structure of a CFC, arguments, parameters, and encapsulating information.

Chapter 2, Effective Component Development highlights some important attributes and techniques to optimize your component's output. We also investigate introspecting a component as well as providing and reading metadata.

Chapter 3, Building Your First Bean begins the reader's journey into object-oriented development. This chapter focuses on a Bean object, understanding requirements and benefits for using one, and how to set and access properties within the Bean.

Chapter 4, Inheritance and Object-Oriented Concepts starts to explore the world of object-oriented programming in a little more detail. This chapter also introduces some key concepts such as polymorphism and composition.

Chapter 5, Data Access Objects looks at the use of Data Access Objects to access and obtain information from a data source. We'll also look at persisting objects in memory throughout your application.

Chapter 6, Gateways introduces an optional data access method for use in your object-oriented development, and also highlights some extra benefits of code separation to help enable easier code management within your applications.

Chapter 7, Creating a Service Layer introduces the use of facade objects to your application's underlying API / component structure. We also explore object inheritance and options to streamline the existing code within your framework.

What you need for this book

To get the most out of this publication, you will require version 8 or 9 of the ColdFusion server. You will also need a SQL database such as SQL server or MySQL to create a database to run the code examples.

Conventions

In this book, you will find a number of styles of text that distinguish between different kinds of information. Here are some examples of these styles, and an explanation of their meaning.

Code words in text are shown as follows: "Let's take a look at the onApplicatonStart() method as it currently stands within the Application.cfc file."

A block of code is set as follows:

```
<cfscript>
objProjects = createObject("component", "com.projects.Projects");
</cfscript>
<cfoutput>
The current date is #objProjects.getCurrentDate()#
</cfoutput>
```

When we wish to draw your attention to a particular part of a code block, the relevant lines or items are set in bold:

```
<cffunction name="getAllUsers" access="public" output="false"
  hint="I run a query of all users within the database table.">
  <!--- Call the query method from the User Gateway and return the
    query object. --->
  <cfreturn variables.instance.userGW.filterAllUsers() />
</cffunction>
```

New terms and **important words** are shown in bold. Words that you see on the screen, in menus or dialog boxes for example, appear in the text like this: "clicking the **Next** button moves you to the next screen".

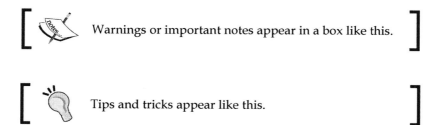

Warnings or important notes appear in a box like this.

Tips and tricks appear like this.

Reader feedback

Feedback from our readers is always welcome. Let us know what you think about this book—what you liked or may have disliked. Reader feedback is important for us to develop titles that you really get the most out of.

To send us general feedback, simply send an e-mail to feedback@packtpub.com, and mention the book title via the subject of your message.

If there is a book that you need and would like to see us publish, please send us a note in the **SUGGEST A TITLE** form on www.packtpub.com or e-mail suggest@packtpub.com.

If there is a topic that you have expertise in and you are interested in either writing or contributing to a book, see our author guide on www.packtpub.com/authors.

Customer support

Now that you are the proud owner of a Packt book, we have a number of things to help you to get the most from your purchase.

Downloading the example code for this book

You can download the example code files for all Packt books you have purchased from your account at http://www.PacktPub.com. If you purchased this book elsewhere, you can visit http://www.PacktPub.com/support and register to have the files e-mailed directly to you.

Errata

Although we have taken every care to ensure the accuracy of our content, mistakes do happen. If you find a mistake in one of our books—maybe a mistake in the text or the code—we would be grateful if you would report this to us. By doing so, you can save other readers from frustration and help us improve subsequent versions of this book. If you find any errata, please report them by visiting http://www.packtpub.com/support, selecting your book, clicking on the **errata submission form** link, and entering the details of your errata. Once your errata are verified, your submission will be accepted and the errata will be uploaded on our website, or added to any list of existing errata, under the Errata section of that title. Any existing errata can be viewed by selecting your title from http://www.packtpub.com/support.

Piracy

Piracy of copyright material on the Internet is an ongoing problem across all media. At Packt, we take the protection of our copyright and licenses very seriously. If you come across any illegal copies of our works, in any form, on the Internet, please provide us with the location address or website name immediately so that we can pursue a remedy.

Please contact us at copyright@packtpub.com with a link to the suspected pirated material.

We appreciate your help in protecting our authors, and our ability to bring you valuable content.

Questions

You can contact us at questions@packtpub.com if you are having a problem with any aspect of the book, and we will do our best to address it.

1
Introducing ColdFusion Components

ColdFusion Components, commonly known as CFCs, were introduced in ColdFusion MX. In essence, they are simple templates written in existing CFML tags and CFScript. As such, they are not complex, confusing, or difficult to understand. If you can code CFML, you can create CFCs.

In this chapter, we will cover the following:

- The basic structure of a ColdFusion component
- The component tags, functions, and methods
- Passing parameters using the argument scope

For those with any experience with ColdFusion, components should be relatively commonplace. Object-Oriented Programming (OOP) relies heavily on the use of ColdFusion components, so before proceeding onto the ins and outs of OOP, let's re-familiarize ourselves with components within ColdFusion. This introduction will also serve as a reference when looking at subjects later in the book.

ColdFusion Components use the same ColdFusion Markup Language (CFML) as 'standard' ColdFusion pages. The core difference is the file extension—components must be saved with a `.cfc` file extension as opposed to the `.cfm` file extensions for template pages.

The basic structure of a ColdFusion Component is:

- The **component** (the page within which you create the code to hold data or perform functions)
- The **methods** available to run within the CFC, also known as **functions**

In simple terms, CFCs themselves form a framework within ColdFusion, allowing you to write structured, clear, and organized code. They make application development easier to manage, control, and maintain.

 ColdFusion Components use the same CFML as 'standard' ColdFusion pages. The core difference is the file extension.

Why use CFCs?

It is not unusual for applications to grow and seem overly complex. Pages containing detailed information, such as business logic, data access and manipulation, data validation, and layout/presentation logic, can become untidy and hard to manage.

Creating and developing applications using CFCs enables you to separate the code logic from the design and presentation, and build an application based around, if not using, traditional **Model View Controller (MVC)** framework methodologies.

Utilizing CFCs and creating a clear structured format for your code will help reduce the complexity of logic within your pages and improve the application speed. Having a clearly structured, well organized code base will make it easier to develop as an individual and share resources within a team. This is the instant benefit of CFC development.

A well-written CFC will allow you to reuse your functions, or methods, across your entire application, helping to reduce the risk of code duplication. It will keep your component libraries and code base to a more easily manageable size, preventing it from becoming convoluted and difficult to follow.

ColdFusion components are an incredibly powerful and valuable means of creating efficient code. They allow you to:

- Share properties and variables between other methods and functions
- Share and interact with functions contained within other CFCs
- Inherit the properties and methods of a base component
- Overwrite methods and functions within other components

CFCs also give you the ability to clearly document and comment your code, letting you and other developers know what each function and property should do, what it should be expecting to receive to do the job and what output it will give you. ColdFusion components are able to read themselves and display this data to you, using a form of **introspection**, which we will cover in *Chapter 2*.

Although CFCs are an effective tool for code reuse, this is not to say they should be used for every reusable function within your application. They are not a complete replacement for custom tags and user-defined functions.

When you load a CFC (instantiate the component), this uses up more processing time than it would to call a custom tag or a User-Defined Function (**UDF**) into use. Once a CFC has been instantiated, however, calling a method or function within the component will take approximately the same time as it would to call a UDF.

It is important, therefore, that CFCs should not necessarily be used as a complete replacement for any UDFs or custom tags that you have in your application. Any code you write can, of course, be optimized, and changes can be made as you learn new things, but UDFs and custom tags perform perfectly well. Using them as they are will help to keep any processing overheads on your application to a minimum.

Grouping your functions

You may have already written custom tags and user-defined functions that allow similar functionality and reusability, for example, a series of UDFs that interact with a shopping cart. By grouping your functions within specific components according to their use and purpose, you can successfully keep your code library organized and more efficient.

You can also further clean your code library by compiling or grouping multiple related components into a package, clearly named and stored in a directory within your application.

Organizing your components

A typical method for organizing your CFC library is to create a directory structure based on your company or domain name, followed by a directory whose name references the purpose of the included components, for example, 'com. coldfumonkeh.projecttracker' in the webroot of your application.

Within this directory, you would then create a directory for each group (or package), of components, with a name reflecting or matching the component name and purpose.

Use your ColdFusion Components to create a component structure, or a library, that contains grouped methods and functions, particularly if the methods share properties or data.

The ColdFusion component tags

You can use these following tags to create a ColdFusion Component.

Tag	Purpose
cfcomponent	The core CFC tag that defines the component structure. All other content in the component is wrapped within this tag.
cffunction	Creates a method (function) within the component.
cfargument	Creates a parameter, otherwise known as an argument, to be sent to the function.
cfproperty	Can be used to define and document the properties within your component. Can also be used to define variables within a CFC that is used as a web service.

These previously mentioned tags are written within the .cfc file that defines the ColdFusion component.

In the world of object-oriented programming, you will commonly hear or see reference to the word 'Class'. A class is essentially a blueprint that is used to instantiate an object, and typically contains methods and instance variables.

When discussing a Class in the context of ColdFusion development, we are basically referencing a ColdFusion component, so when you see or read about classes, remember it is essentially an alias for a CFC.

Our first component

To get started, in this example, we will create a component and functions to output the message "Hello world".

Create a new file called greetings.cfc and save it within your ColdFusion webroot.

The following is a component base tag; add this code into the new CFC to define the component:

```
<cfcomponent displayName="greetings">
</cfcomponent>
```

Listing 1.1 – component base tags

As you can see, the name attribute within the CFC matches the name of the file. The `cfcomponent` tags form the base structure of our ColdFusion Component. No other code can be placed outside of these tags, as it will simply display an error.

It may be helpful to think of the `cfcomponent` tag as the wrapping paper on a parcel. It forms the outer shell of the package, holding everything else nicely in place.

Defining a method

We have now created the component, but at the moment it does not actually do anything. It has no function to run. We need to add a method into the CFC to create a function to call and use within our application. The following code is a basic function definition; place it between the opening and closing `cfcomponent` tags:

```
<cffunction name="sayHello">
  <!--- the CFML code for the method will go here --->
</cffunction>
```

Listing 1.2 – basic function definition

You have now added a method to the CFC. The `cffunction` tags are nested within the `cfcomponent` tags. We now need to add some CFML code within the `cffunction` tags to create our method and perform the operation. Let's create a variable within the function that will be our display message. The following code is for declaring a string variable; place it inside the `cffunction` tags:

```
<cffunction name="sayHello">
  <cfset var strHelloMessage = 'Hello World!' />
</cffunction>
```

Listing 1.3 – declaring a string variable

We have created a string variable containing the text to display to the browser.

Returning the data

To return the data we need to add an extra tag into the method. This is possible by using the `cfreturn` tag, which returns results from a component method. The `cfreturn` tag has one required attribute that is the expression or value you wish to return.

Add the following code to your CFC so our method will return the welcome message and the completed component will look like this:

```
<cfcomponent displayName="greetings">
  <cffunction name="sayHello">
```

```
        <cfset var strHelloMessage = 'Hello World!' />
        <cfreturn strHelloMessage />
    </cffunction>
</cfcomponent>
```

Listing 1.4 – returning data from the function

ColdFusion 9 scripted components

Since the release of ColdFusion 9, developers now have the ability to also write ColdFusion components in complete script syntax instead of pure tag form.

To write the previous component in this format, the code would look as follows:

```
component
  displayname="greetings"
  {
    function sayHello(){
      // the CFML code for the method will go here
      var strHelloMessage='Hello World';
      return strHelloMessage;
    }
  }
```

Listing 1.5 – component declaration in the script syntax

Although written using cfscript syntax, there is no requirement to wrap the code within <cfscript> tags, instead we can write it directly within the .cfc page.

We do not even need to contain the code within cfcomponent tags, as the entire content of the component will be compiled as cfscript if left as plain text without tags.

Creating your object

There it is, a simple ColdFusion Component. The method is created using the cffunction tags, wrapped up nicely within the cfcomponent tags, and the value returned using the cfreturn tag. Now that we have written the function, how do we call it?

In this example, we will call the component and run the method by using the **createObject()** function. Create a new file called hello.cfm and add the following code to the template:

```
<cfset objGreeting = createObject('component', 'greetings') />
<cfoutput>#objGreeting.sayHello()#</cfoutput>
```

Listing 1.6 – creating the component object

In the previous code, we have created an instance of the greetings CFC, which we can reference by using the `objGreeting` variable. We have then accessed the `sayHello()` method within the component, surrounded by `cfoutput` tags, to display the returned data.

Save the file and view it within your browser. You should now see the welcome message that we created within the method.

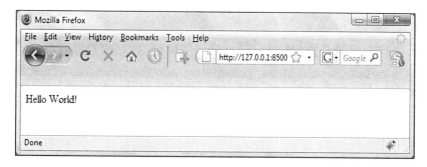

Restricting your functions to scopes

Imagine we are sending some data through to a login page in our application within the URL scope; the first and last name of a particular person. On the page, we want to join the two values and combine them into one string to form the individual's full name. We could write the code directly on the page, as follows:

```
<cfoutput>
   Hello, #URL.firstName# #URL.lastName#
</cfoutput>
```

Listing 1.7 – displaying URL variables as a string

Although this works, you can revise the code and transform it into a ColdFusion function to concatenate the two values into the required single string and return that value:

```
<cffunction name="getName">
   <cfset var strFullName = URL.firstName & ' ' & URL.lastName />
   <cfreturn strFullName />
</cffunction>
```

Listing 1.8 – concatenate variables into string

You can then call this function within your `.cfm` page to output the resulting string from the function:

```
<cfoutput>
   #getName()#
</cfoutput>
```

However, within this code you have restricted yourself to using only the specific URL scope. What if the first name and last name values were in the FORM scope, or pulled from a query? This block of code is useful only for values within the form scope.

Using arguments within your methods

To allow us to be able to pass in any parameters into the `getName()` function, we need to use the `cfargument` tag to send data into the method. By changing the function in the following code example, the method will create the concatenated string and produce the same results from two parameters or arguments that you choose to pass in.

```
<cffunction name="getName">
  <cfargument name="firstName" type="string" />
  <cfargument name="lastName" type="string" />
    <cfset var strFullName = arguments.firstName & '
       ' & arguments.lastName />
  <cfreturn strFullName />
</cffunction>
```

Listing 1.10 – using arguments within your function

The `cfargument` tag creates a parameter definition within the component method, and allows you to send in arguments for inclusion into the functions.

The Arguments scope

The `Arguments` scope only exists in a method. The scope contains any variables that you have passed into that method, and you can access the variables within the `Arguments` scope in the following ways:

- using structure notation - `Arguments.variablename` or `Arguments["variablename"]`
- using array notation - `Arguments[1]`

The Arguments scope does not persist between calls to available CFC methods, meaning that you cannot access a value within the Arguments scope in one function from inside a different function.

Redefine the function parameters

By defining two arguments and sending in the values for the first and last names, you have created an unrestricted function that is not tied to a specific scope or set of hardcoded values. You can instead choose what values to pass into it on your calling page:

```
<cfoutput>
  #getName('Gary', 'Brown')#
</cfoutput>
```

Lsiting 1.11a – sending parameters into our function

Now that we have removed any restrictions to the values we pass in, and taken away any references to hardcoded variables, we can reuse this function, sending in whichever values or variables we choose to. For example, we could use variables from the FORM scope, URL scope, or query items to concatenate the string:

```
<cfoutput>
  #getName(form.firstName, form.lastName)#
</cfoutput>
```

Listing 1.11b – sending parameters into our function

Let's take our getName() method and add it into the greeting.cfc file. By doing so, we are grouping two methods that have a similarity in purpose into one component. This is good programming practice and will aid in creating manageable and clearly organized code.

Our greeting.cfc should now look like this:

```
<cfcomponent name="greetings">
  <cffunction name="sayHello">
    <cfset var strHelloMessage = 'Hello World!' />
    <cfreturn strHelloMessage />
  </cffunction>
  <cffunction name="getName">
    <cfargument name="firstName" type="string" />
    <cfargument name="lastName" type="string" />
      <cfset var strFullName = arguments.firstName & '
        ' & arguments.lastName />
```

```
        <cfreturn strFullName />
    </cffunction>
</cfcomponent>
```

Listing 1.12 – `revised greeting.cfc`

Combining your methods

As we have seen, you can easily access the methods within a defined CFC and output the data in a `.cfm` template page.

You can also easily access the functionality of one method in a CFC from another method. This is particularly useful when your component definition contains grouped functions that may have a relationship based upon their common purpose.

To show this, let's create a new method that will use the results from both of our existing functions within the `greetings.cfc` file. Instead of displaying a generic "Hello World" message, we will incorporate the returned data from the `getName()` method and display a personalized greeting.

Create a new method within the CFC, called personalGreeting.

```
<cffunction name="personalGreeting">
    <cfargument name="firstName" type="string" />
    <cfargument name="lastName" type="string" />
        <cfscript>
            strHello = sayHello();
            strFullName = getName(firstName=arguments.firstName,
                lastName=arguments.lastName);
            strHelloMessage = strHello & ' My name is ' & strFullName;
        </cfscript>
    <cfreturn strHelloMessage />
</cffunction>
```

Listing 1.13 – `personalGreeting` method

Within this method, we are calling our two previously defined methods. The returned value from the `sayHello()` method is being stored as a string variable, "strHello".

We then retrieve the returned value from the `getName()` method and store this in a string variable "strFullName". As we have written the `getName()` function to accept two arguments to form the concatenated name string, we also need to add the same two arguments to the `personalGreeting()` method, as done in the previous code. They will then be passed through to the `getName()` method in exactly the same way as if we were calling that function directly.

Using the two variables that now hold the returned data, we create our `strHelloMessage` variable, which joins the two values, and is then returned from the method using the `cfreturn` tag.

In this method, we used CFScript instead of CFML and `cfset` tags, which were used in our previous functions. There is no hard and fast rule for this. You can use whichever coding method you find the most comfortable.

Let's call this method on our `hello.cfm` template page, using the following code:

```
<!--- instatiate the component --->
<cfset objGreeting = createObject('component', 'greetings') />
<!--- access the method and assign results to a string --->
<cfset strPersonalGreeting = objGreeting.personalGreeting(
  firstName="Gary", lastName="Brown") />
<cfoutput>#strPersonalGreeting#</cfoutput>
```

Listing 1.14 – calling the `personalGreeting` method

We are sending in the same arguments that we were passing through to the original `getName()` method, in the same way. This time we are passing these through using the newly created `personalGreeting()` method.

You should now see a personalized greeting message displayed in your browser:

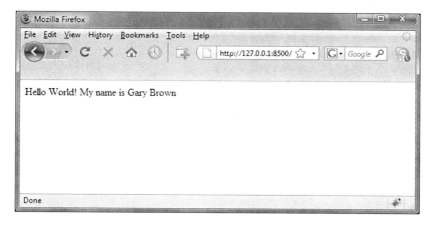

Protecting your local variables

In our previous `personalGreeting()` method, we included two separate functions, `sayHello()` and `getName()`, into the main method. This is not an uncommon practice, and is what you would expect when writing detailed components with relationships between its included functions.

One issue that can arise when developing in this way is when two or more methods contain a variable of the same name and the value of that variable is accessed or changed by one of the methods.

As an example, the following code contains two functions, baseNumber() and multiplyNumbers().

While the cfcomponent tag has been excluded in this example, this could also easily be turned into a CFC by wrapping the functions within cfcomponent tags.

```
<cfoutput>
<cffunction name="baseNumber" returnType="numeric">
  <cfargument name="a" type="numeric" required="true" />
    <cfset x = arguments.a />
  <cfreturn x />
</cffunction>
<cffunction name="multiplyNumbers" returntype="string">
  <cfargument name="a" type="numeric" required="true" />
  <cfargument name="b" type="numeric" required="true" />

    <!--- multiply our basenumber value by 10 --->
    <cfset x = 10 />
    <cfset y = baseNumber(a) />
  <cfreturn y & " multiplied by " & x & " = " & x * arguments.b />
</cffunction>
<cfloop from="1" to="10" index="i">
  #multiplyNumbers(i,i)#<br />
</cfloop>
</cfoutput>
```

Listing 1.15 – two user-defined functions

A cfloop tag runs a loop from 1 to 10. The multiplyNumbers() function accepts two arguments. In this example, these are both the index numbers of the loop. We want to multiply our baseNumber value (argument 'a'), by 10 for each loop, creating a 10 times table list. To do this, the multiplyNumbers() function has a hardcoded value (x) that is set to the value of 10.

The desired results you would expect from this code should be:

```
1 multiplied by 10 = 10
2 multiplied by 10 = 20
```

However, this is not the case. If you save the code to a .cfm template and run it in your browser, you will get the following result:

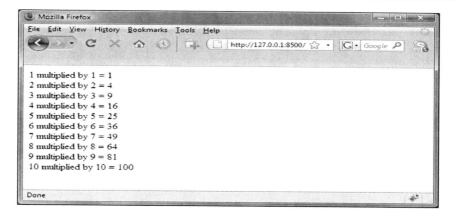

This is clearly not the result you would expect. So what's happening to cause this issue? Let's take another look at our two functions:

```
<cffunction name="baseNumber" returnType="numeric">
  <cfargument name="a" type="numeric" required="true" />
    <cfset x = arguments.a />
  <cfreturn x />
</cffunction>


<cffunction name="multiplyNumbers" returntype="string">
  <cfargument name="a" type="numeric" required="true" />
  <cfargument name="b" type="numeric" required="true" />
    <!--- multiply our basenumber value by 10 --->
    <cfset x = 10 />
    <cfset y = baseNumber(a) />
  <cfreturn y & " multiplied by " & x & " = " & x * arguments.b />
</cffunction>
```

Listing 1.16 – examining the two methods

You can see that both functions have a variable called x. The baseNumber() function stores the value of the argument as the x variable, which it returns into the multiplyNumbers() function for use in the equation. The multiplyNumbers() function also has a variable called x, which is the hardcoded number we wish to use as a multiplier, in this case 10.

Within the function, the returned value from the baseNumber() method is assigned to y for use in the equation, but as this included function is run, it overwrites the value of the hardcoded x variable with its own x value. This, in turn, is passed into the equation, which throws off the expected results.

In the previous example, the x value in both functions is public, meaning that it can be altered or overwritten by any included functions, or if in a CFC, any defined method within the component. They are, in essence, set as 'open' variables that can be accessed and amended.

By running the two functions in this way, with openly accessible variables, it has the effect of ruining our ten times table. Imagine that we had a method controlling the shopping cart in an e-commerce application, updating quantities and costs, perhaps even stock levels of products. If we left these public variables open, they could be accessed by any included functions, and the values could change dramatically altering our shopping cart and its data.

Using the Var scope

To avoid this issue, the best practice is to set any local function variables to only be accessed by that particular function. This is achieved by using the Var keyword when setting variables. By applying variable to the Var scope, you are restricting public access to them and declaring that they are only accessible within the method in which they are defined. This removes any chance that external functions will corrupt the values.

 You should always use the Var keyword on variables that are used only inside of the function in which they are declared.

Let's alter our code to include the Var keyword to ensure the variables are available only to the functions in which they are written:

```
<cffunction name="baseNumber" returnType="numeric">
  <cfargument name="a" type="numeric" required="true" />
    <cfset Var x = arguments.a />
  <cfreturn x />
</cffunction>

<cffunction name="multiplyNumbers" returntype="string">
  <cfargument name="a" type="numeric" required="true" />
  <cfargument name="b" type="numeric" required="true" />
    <cfset Var x = 10 />
    <cfset var y = baseNumber(a) />
  <cfreturn y & " multiplied by " & x & " = " & x * arguments.b />
</cffunction>
```

Listing 1.17 – Var scoping our variables

If we save the code with the `Var` keyword applied to the variables and view the page in the browser, you will now see the correct results displayed:

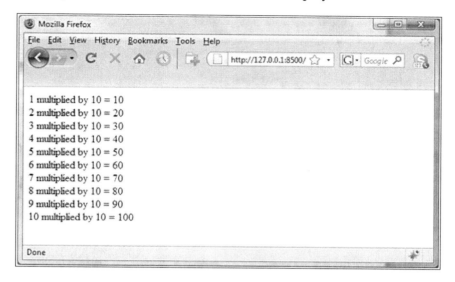

Regardless of the type of variable you are using within your component methods, (a query, string, integer, array, or structure) if it is used only within the function in which it is declared, it needs to be `Var` scoped to protect it and to avoid any unwanted amendments by other functions.

Placing your Var scoped variables

Up to ColdFusion 8, all `Var` scoped variables were required to be placed after any arguments within the function (if there are any included), and before any CFML.

Enhancements in ColdFusion 9 removed this restriction, and `Var` scoped variables can be placed anywhere within a code block or function.

Naming your Var scoped variables

While there are no strict conventions when naming your `Var` scoped variables, be aware that a naming conflict will arise if your local variable name is the same as any defined argument name (or the name of another local variable).

```
<cffunction name="baseNumber" returnType="numeric">
  <cfargument name="x" type="numeric" required="true" />
    <cfset Var x = arguments.x />
  <cfreturn x />
</cffunction>
```

Listing 1.18 – `baseNumber` function

For example, if we have written the `baseNumber()` method as in the previous code, with the argument and local variable both called x, this would display an error, as a local variable within a function cannot be declared twice.

Accessing your CFC

Once you are ready to use your CFCs, you need to access the methods placed within. There are two ways to access a CFC:

- object instantiation
- invoking the CFC

Instantiating the object

When you instantiate a CFC, you create an instance of the component. This instance preserves the data within the CFC for as long as it exists. You would typically create an instance of a component at the top of the page. By doing so, you would have access to its methods and functions on the entire page, without having to create a new instance for each call.

There are three methods available to you to create an instance of the CFC:

- createObject
- cfobject
- using the NEW operator in ColdFusion 9

Using the createObject function

As used in our earlier examples, the `createObject()` function creates and returns a ColdFusion object.

```
<cfscript>
  objGreeting = createObject('component', 'greetings');
</cfscript>
```

Listing 1.19

Here, we are creating a new instance of the "greetings" component. The first parameter tells the `createObject()` function that we want a component, and the second references the name of the component of which we want to create an instance.

While the CFC is in the same directory as the calling page, in the previous example, if we had the CFC within a different directory in the webroot, for example, a folder named components; this second parameter would read as follows:

```
createObject('component', 'components.greetings');
```

This is because the second parameter is a dot notation representation of the path to the component.

Using the cfobject tag

Similar to the createObject() function, the cfobject tag has three attributes.

```
<cfobject name="greetingsObject" component="greetings"
  type="component" />
```

Listing 1.20

The name attribute defines the name of the returned variable of the CFC instance so you can access the component to use your methods. The component attribute represents a dot notation path to the CFC you wish to instantiate. The third attribute, type, is optional, and has the default value component.

Using the NEW operator

The enhancements in ColdFusion 9 now provide an alternative way of creating an instance of a component object without using the createObject() function.

We can now create the object through the use of the new operator, like so:

```
<cfscript>
  // create the object
  objGreeting = new greeting();
</cfscript>
```

Listing 1.21

Using cfinvoke

You can invoke your component and access the method simultaneously by using the cfinvoke tag. When you invoke (call) the CFC using this tag, you are not creating an instance of the component that will be preserved and available for use elsewhere within your CFML page. Instead, you are creating an instance of the CFC that comes into existence as soon as you invoke the method, and ceases to exist as soon as the requested method has returned a result.

In essence, you are bringing the component to life long enough to get the details you need from it and closing it down as soon as the information is returned.

The cfinvoke tag

Let's make a call to our `sayHello()` method within the `greetings.cfc` component.

Add the following code to your `hello.cfm` template page:

```
<cfinvoke component="greetings" method="sayHello"
   returnVariable="strHello" />
<cfoutput>#strHello#</cfoutput>
```

Listing 1.22

Here, we are invoking the greetings component, selecting the method within the CFC that we want to access, (in this case the `sayHello()` function) and assigning a variable (`strHello`), to which the returned data will be saved for us to access it within the page.

Outputting the `returnVariable` onto the page will provide us with the same result as we have seen before.

Using cfinvokeargument

The `cfinvoke` tag also allows us to pass in parameters to the methods we are calling, by means of the `cfinvokeargument` tag.

```
<cfinvoke component="greetings" method="personalGreeting"
   returnVariable="strPersonalGreeting">
   <cfinvokeargument name="firstName" value="Matt" />
   <cfinvokeargument name="lastName" value="James" />
</cfinvoke>
```

Listing 1.23

We are sending our parameters used in the `personalGreeting()` method in a similar format to the `cfargument` tag, using the `cfinvokeargument` tag, which is nested within the `cfinvoke` tag. The `cfinvokeargument` tag takes the name and value of the argument and sends it into the method you are calling.

Using attributes as arguments

Alternatively, when using the `cfinvoke` tag, you can send through the parameters as named attribute-value pairs, providing one attribute per argument.

```
<cfinvoke component="greetings" method="personalGreeting"
   firstName="Gary" lastName="Brown"
   returnVariable="strPersonalGreeting" />
```

Listing 1.24

You can see in the previous code that the firstName and lastName parameters are written as attributes within the cfinvoke tag itself.

Using an argument collection

The optional argumentCollection attribute for the cfinvoke tag accepts a structure in the form of an associative array of arguments to pass into the method.

```
<cfscript>
   // create a structure to hold the values
   stuArguments = structNew();
   stuArguments.firstName = "James";
   stuArguments.lastName = "Brown";
</cfscript>
<cfinvoke component="greetings" method="personalGreeting"
   argumentCollection="#stuArguments#"
   returnVariable="strPersonalGreeting" />
```

Listing 1.25

The structure names must match the names of the arguments within the method.

Passing arguments into an instance method call

As you have seen in the previous examples, we have sent parameters into the methods on our pages. There are two options available to send your arguments into your method call on an instantiated object.

As a list

You can send the two arguments through as a comma-delimited list. If you use this option, the order of the parameters you pass into the function call must match the order of arguments defined within the method.

In our `personalGreeting()` function the first name is the first argument, and the last name is the second argument, therefore you would do the following to call the method:

```
<cfset strPersonalGreeting =
  objGreeting.personalGreeting("Daft","Vader") />
```

Listing 1.26

As named values

An alternative method of sending arguments into a function is to use named values. This option ensures that the values passed through are assigned to the correct argument within the method. This means you do not have to place the parameters within the function call in any specific order, as the name of the parameter will match the name of the argument within the method.

```
<cfset strPersonalGreeting =
  objGreeting.personalGreeting(firstName="Daft",lastName="Vader") />
```

Listing 1.27

As an argumentCollection

As mentioned earlier, we also have the ability to send arguments through to the method using the `argumentCollection` attribute, and send through a structure of values.

Arguments in action

Let's look at another simple use case for creating reusable components and functions, which will also highlight some benefits of passing arguments into your methods.

Merging your functions into one

Create a new CFC called `contacts.cfc`, and add your `cfcomponent` tags to define the component.

Add the following method in the `contacts.cfc` file. This new function runs a SELECT query on the Project Tracker application database to retrieve a recordset of all contacts:

```
<cffunction name="getContacts">
  <cfset var rstContacts = "" />
```

```
    <cfquery name="rstContacts" datasource="projectTracker">
    SELECT firstName,lastName FROM Owners
    </cfquery>
    <cfreturn rstContacts />
</cffunction>
```

Listing 1.28

We now have a function returning our query data. We also want to have a query to pull out a specific record based on the record ID of a particular person.

We can create a second function to handle this as well:

```
<cffunction name="getContact">
  <cfargument name="ID" type="numeric" />
  <cfset var rstContact = "" />
  <cfquery name="rstContact" datasource="projectTracker">
    SELECT firstName,lastName FROM Owners
      WHERE ID = <cfqueryparam cfsqltype="cf_sql_integer"
      value="#arguments.ID#" />
  </cfquery>
  <cfreturn rstContact />
</cffunction>
```

Listing 1.29

These two methods within the `contacts.cfc` file interact with our database and return query data. However, the two queries pull out exactly the same information from the database. The only difference between the queries is that `getContact()` returns records for a specific user, based upon the ID value. We can easily streamline our CFC by combining these two methods into one, which will remove unnecessary code from our files and theoretically turn one function into two.

Using cfargument to combine your methods

In this example, we will combine the two SELECT queries into one method, using the `cfargument` tag.

```
<cffunction name="getContact">
  <cfargument name="ID" type="numeric" default="0" />
  <cfset var rstContact = "" />
  <cfquery name="rstContact" datasource="projectTracker">
    SELECT firstName,lastName FROM Owners
    <cfif arguments.ID GT 0>
      WHERE ID = <cfqueryparam cfsqltype="cf_sql_integer"
        value="#arguments.ID#" />
```

```
        </cfif>
      </cfquery>
      <cfreturn rstContact />
    </cffunction>
```

Listing 1.30

The `cfargument` tag has a `default` attribute, which allows you to provide a default value for an argument if you do not pass one into the method. As the customer ID parameter type is set to "numeric", we have set the default value of the argument to "0". This value will now always be available within our method and will stay at the default value until a parameter is passed in to the function.

By providing a default value, we are now able to wrap a `cfif` tag block around the WHERE clause of the query. If the value of `arguments.ID` (the value of the parameter within the arguments scope) is greater than 0, that is, if we have passed a numeric value into the method ourselves, then include the WHERE clause when running the SQL within the `cfquery` tags.

By doing this, we have merged the two methods within the `contacts.cfc` into one, optimizing our code and allowing it to perform more than one function.

Let's run this query. Create a new page template called `query.cfm`, and paste in the following code to create the object and run the method without sending in any parameters:

```
<!--- instantiate the object --->
<cfset objContacts = createObject('component', 'contacts') />
<!--- dump the results --->
<cfdump var="#objContacts.getContact()#" />
```

Listing 1.31

If no ID value is sent through as a parameter, meaning the default value is 0, the method will return the full recordset of all content from the Owners database table:

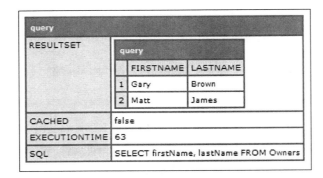

Amend the code by adding in a numeric value to pass through as the ID argument:

```
<!--- dump the results --->
<cfdump var="#objContacts.getContact(2)#" />
```

Listing 1.32

If we provide an ID within the argument, the method will only return the row for the contact that has the matching ID value:

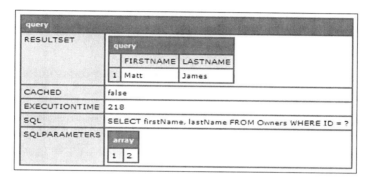

The dumped object now shows us the parameter sent through in the arguments scope and the SQL query that now includes the WHERE clause.

The simple solution of using an argument with a default value and a `cfif` statement to control the flow has streamlined and reduced the amount of extraneous code within your application.

Creating an object constructor

In our `contacts.cfc`, we have defined a method which contains a query. This query has the datasource name attribute defined to correctly reference the database setup within the ColdFusion administration console.

As with all good development, we want to restrict hardcoding any values or references wherever we can and instead use variables to define them, (in this case the datasource name attribute).

A common practice in application development is to create your datasource name and store it in the Application scope, ensuring its availability to every page template that is called, for example:

```
<cfset application.dsn = "projectTracker" />
```

You could use the `Application` scope variable `application.dsn` directly within your CFCs as the dynamic name referencing the datasource. However, this is not considered best coding practice, as you have instantly opened up your component methods to a fixed scope variable.

One of the main goals in component development is to create closed CFCs and methods that do not need to worry about whether or not a fixed variable exists.

If we refer back to the `getName()` function on page 7, we can see how it was originally fixed to read the first and last name from the URL scope. We resolved that issue by removing any fixed scope references and optimized the method by adding `cfargument` tags and the ability to pass in parameters.

We will do the same for our `contacts.cfc` to send in our datasource name for use in the `cfquery` tags.

Instead of creating a new argument for each method within the component that requires the datasource, we will create a new function that will hold the variables we need and will be open for all methods defined within the CFC to read variables from.

Creating an init() function

Let's modify our code within the `contacts.cfc` gallery to write the new function, `init()`.

```
<cfcomponent name="contacts">

  <cffunction name="init">
  <cfargument name="datasource" type="string" required="true" />
    <cfscript>
      Variables.attributes = structNew();
      Variables.attributes.dsn = arguments.datasource;
    </cfscript>
    <cfreturn this />
  </cffunction>

  <cffunction name="getContact">
    <cfargument name="ID" type="numeric" default="0" />
    <cfset var rstContact = "" />
    <cfquery name="rstContact" datasource="projectTracker">
      SELECT firstName,lastName FROM Owners
      <cfif arguments.ID GT 0>
        WHERE ID = <cfqueryparam cfsqltype="cf_sql_integer"
          value="#arguments.ID#" />
      </cfif>
    </cfquery>
    <cfreturn rstContact />
```

```
    </cffunction>
  </cfcomponent>
```

Listing 1.33

You can now see the `init()` method defined within the component. The concept of a constructor within an object is a common practice in most languages. We have included a `cfargument` tag with the name `datasource`, which will allow us to send in the name of the datasource we wish to use within this object.

Within the CFScript block, we then create a new structure that assigns the value of the datasource argument to the struct value `dsn`, and the structure has been assigned to the `Variables` scope within the CFC.

We can then amend our `getContact()` method and alter the datasource attribute to use the new reference, stored in the `Variables` scope:

```
<cffunction name="getContact">
  <cfargument name="ID" type="numeric" default="0" />
    <cfset var rstContact = "" />
      <cfquery name="rstContact"
        datasource="#variables.attributes.dsn#">
        SELECT firstName,lastName FROM Owners
        <cfif arguments.ID GT 0>
          WHERE ID = <cfqueryparam cfsqltype="cf_sql_integer"
            value="#arguments.ID#" />
        </cfif>
      </cfquery>
    <cfreturn rstContact />
</cffunction>
```

Listing 1.34

By sending the value into the object constructor method when instantiating the component we have removed the hardcoded reference to the datasource.

The Variables scope

The `Variables` scope can be made available to the entire CFC by setting a value either within one of the methods or in the constructor. The value of that variable is then made available to any other method (including the constructor).

The `Variables` scope can be used in a similar way to storing values within the `Application` scope, whose values are always available throughout the entire application. This makes it ideal for sending in variables such as the datasource name.

Calling your init() function

To set the value of the datasource name into the `Variables` scope, we need to call the init function to pass through the argument.

In previous examples, we have already used the `createObject()` function to create an instance of the component. We are going to use exactly the same code, only this time we will append the `init()` function to the end of instantiation method call:

```
<!--- instantiate the object --->
<cfset objContacts = createObject('component',
  'contacts').init(datasource="projectTracker") />
```

Listing 1.35

By doing this, we have passed our datasource name as an argument into the `init()` method within the `contacts.cfc`. The argument value is then stored within the `Variables` scope structure (`Variables.attributes`).

> Values stored within the `Variables` scope last as long as the component instance exists, and therefore can persist between calls to methods of a CFC instance.

The `Variables` scope within your CFC is available to any included pages (using the `cfinclude` tag), and any `Variables` scope variables that you have defined in the included page are also available to the CFC.

The This scope

At the end of the function, we have the `cfreturn` tag, which we have seen before. However, this particular method is returning a different value, which is `This`:

```
<cffunction name="init">
  <cfreturn This />
</cffunction>
```

Listing 1.36

By adding a return type of `This` to the `cfreturn` tag, you are returning the entire object, including all of its methods, variables, and data.

In the `query.cfm` calling page, use the `cfdump` tag to display the object in the browser:

```
<!--- dump the contacts object --->
<cfdump var="#objContacts#" />
```

Listing 1.37

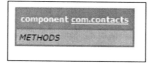

As the `init()` method returns the object in the `This` scope, we are able to access the object directly using the `cfdump` tag.

The `This` scope is similar to the `Variables` scope due to the fact that it is 'globally' accessible to the entire CFC. In addition, the `This` scope is accessible outside of the CFC, so you could call and reference the values from your object within your `.cfm` template calling page.

For example, if we amended the code within the `init()` method in the CFC from using the previously mentioned `Variables` scope to the `This` scope, we could access the datasource name from our calling page:

```
<cffunction name="init">
  <cfargument name="datasource" required="true" />
    <cfscript>
      This.attributes = structNew();
      This.attributes.dsn = arguments.datasource;
    </cfscript>
  <cfreturn This />
</cffunction>
```

Listing 1.38

In the `query.cfm`, we can now output the name of the datasource from the attributes structure stored within the `This` scope:

```
<!--- dump the contacts object --->
<cfdump var="#objContacts#" />
<cfoutput>The datasource name is
  #objContacts.attributes.dsn#</cfoutput>
```

Listing 1.39

Notice that the attributes structure is now publicly available, allowing us to access the name of the datasource directly from the CFC.

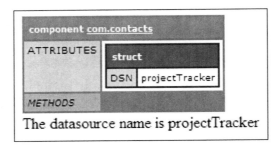

The datasource name is projectTracker

This highlights the difference between the `Variables` and `This` scope. When the attributes were assigned to the `Variables` scope, they were kept hidden from external views, despite being available to all methods within the CFC. As soon as we changed the `init()` method to store attributes within the `This` scope, the structure became a visible, 'public' variable that could be accessed outside of the CFC.

Although the `This` scope is a required tool for returning a complete CFC object, it is not best practice to store variables within the scope. This is because they can be accessed and altered. Unless you specifically choose to alter your object's variables in this manner, this would not be a safe development practice.

 Values stored within the `This` scope last as long as the component instance exists, and therefore can persist between calls to methods of a CFC instance.

Summary

We have looked at ColdFusion Components, what they are and what they are for. Within this chapter, we have also covered:

- The basic structure of a CFC
- The component tags
- Grouping functions and methods
- How to use arguments within your methods
- Optimizing and encapsulating your functions to improve code portability

- Instantiating your objects, as well as creating an object constructor method
- The Arguments, This and Variables scope, and to Var scope function variables

2
Effective Component Development

In this chapter, we will learn about the benefits of including attributes into our components, functions, and arguments within the ColdFusion component.

We will also cover the following topics:

- Using the pseudo-constructor method to set variables
- Whitespace suppression within the CFC
- Returning data from your function
- Access properties and restrictions
- Documentation and introspection
- Creating and reading metadata from the component

Pseudo-constructors

In *Chapter 1, Introducing ColdFusion Components* we looked at how to create an instance of a ColdFusion component using the createObject() function. We also looked at how to pass values through to the instantiated object upon creation using the init() method (also known as the object constructor method), thereby making them available to all methods within the CFC.

You can use any CFML tags or CFScript code within your component document to create your constructor code, and typically it is best practice to place the constructors at the top of the document, directly beneath the opening cfcomponent tag and before any method definitions.

ColdFusion provides an alternative method for setting your CFC-wide variables in your component, using a **pseudo-constructor**. This term simply refers to the code contained within the `cfcomponent` tags but outside of a `cffunction` block.

A pseudo-constructor's role is to set variables, run queries, or run any code during the instantiation of the object.

Using the pseudo method

Let's use a pseudo-constructor in an example. Create a new CFC, called `projects.cfc`, and save the file within your component directory structure, inside a directory called `projects` from your webroot. The path to the `projects.cfc` file should now be `com/projects/projects.cfc`. Place the following sample data within the new file:

```
<cfcomponent name="Projects">
  <!--- pseudo constructor code here --->
  <cfset This.dsn = "projectTracker" />
  Our datasource is #This.dsn#
  <!--- function to get the current date --->
  <cffunction name="getCurrentDate" output="false" returnType="Date">
    <cfreturn dateFormat(Now(), "dd/mm/yyyy") />
  </cffunction>
</cfcomponent>
```

Listing 2.1 – Using the pseudo constructor

We have a method called `getCurrentDate()` that returns the current date. Directly above this function we are setting a `dsn` variable that we can use to reference our datasource name in any included queries. We also have a single line of text (**Our datasource is #This.dsn#**) — all of which form our basic pseudo-constructor code.

Create a new CFM template called `projects.cfm` within the webroot, and place the following code within it to instantiate the object and output the data:

```
<cfscript>
  objProjects = createObject("component", "com.projects.Projects");
</cfscript>
<cfoutput>
  The current date is #objProjects.getCurrentDate()#
</cfoutput>
```

Listing 2.2 – Output the current date

Notice that in this example, we are not using an `init()` method as we have not written one in the component. Instead, we are using the pseudo-constructor to create the variables we need within the object. With the pseudo-constructor setting the `dsn` value, we can create a variable available for use throughout the entire CFC.

Within the `cfoutput` tags, we are returning the value from the `getCurrentDate()` method. Save this page and view it within your browser to check the results.

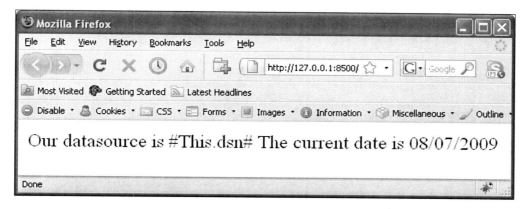

As you would expect, the `getCurrentDate()` method has returned the expected date value, using the ColdFusion `dateFormat()` function.

You may notice in the output from our example that the text we had written at the top of the `projects.cfc` (**Our datasource is #This.dsn#**), has also been written to the browser, although it has not been evaluated as an expression.

This is to highlight the important fact that all code and text within the pseudo-constructor code block will be processed during object instantiation. As we have seen, even standard text can and will be returned from the CFC.

Suppressing whitespace

ColdFusion can generate a lot of unnecessary whitespace from any CFML code. It can also output unwanted text written in a component or method, (in our example, the line of text in the pseudo-constructor).

Luckily, there is a way to reduce any whitespace and to ensure that you display only the variables or data you wish to.

Output attribute

The `output` attribute is an optional Boolean attribute, available for use within the `cfcomponent` and `cffunction` tags. Through its use you are able to dictate the way in which whitespace and data output is managed.

Let's revise our component code by adding in the output attribute to the opening `cfcomponent` tag:

```
<cfcomponent name="Projects" output="false">
  <!--- pseudo constructor code here --->
  <cfset This.dsn = "projectTracker" />
  Our datasource is #This.dsn#
  <!--- function to get the current date --->
  <cffunction name="getCurrentDate" output="false" returnType="Date">
    <cfreturn dateFormat(Now(), "dd/mm/yyyy") />
  </cffunction>
</cfcomponent>
```

Listing 2.3 – Adding the output attribute to `projects.cfc`

By setting the output attribute to `false` at the component level, we have told ColdFusion not to display or output any variables or data within the pseudo-constructor code.

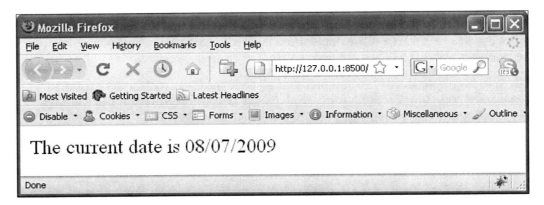

Running the `projects.cfm` page in the browser again will still show the returned string from the `getCurrentDate()`, but the text is no longer visible.

Change the value of the output attribute to true, and run the `projects.cfm` page in the browser again.

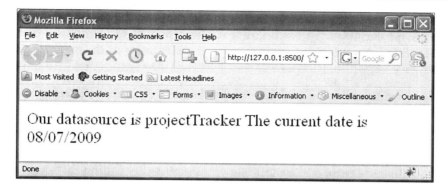

You can now see that the `#This.dsn#` value is being displayed as an evaluated ColdFusion variable, without the need for any `cfoutput` tags.

Notice that the `dsn` variable was stored in the `This` scope within the CFC, to make it visible on the ColdFusion calling page if we wished to call it directly.

As covered in *Chapter 1*, you could restrict external access to this value by setting it to the `Variables` scope within the component. This would ensure that the variable would only be visible to the methods within the CFC, and not any `.cfm` calling pages.

If no output attribute is written in the `cfcomponent` tag, as we had included in our first block of code, ColdFusion displays output from within the pseudo-constructor. It does not evaluate any variables such as the `#This.dsn#` expression. To do so, you would need to wrap expressions within `cfoutput` tags.

The same output attribute, as mentioned, can also be applied to `cffunction` tags to suppress or display any code written within the specific method, and works with exactly the same principle and output rules as mentioned earlier.

It is a good practice to set your output attribute to `false` to avoid generating unnecessary whitespace or returning any extraneous data unless it is the specific requirement of the component or function to do so.

Pseudo-constructor or init() method

We have seen that the pseudo-constructor method is an alternative to the `init()` method as a way of constructing your properties during its instantiation.

However, as shown in the example earlier in the chapter, the pseudo-constructor is unable to accept variables. This is because it is not included in a method that we are able to pass data into. It instead runs as soon as an instance of the object is created. As a result, any variables, such as our `dsn` reference, are hardcoded into the CFC.

This poses a problem. For truly object-oriented code, remember the rules surrounding encapsulation and hardcoding values. We are also unable to dynamically alter the values set within our objects.

The `init()` method was established by the ColdFusion community as the preferred standard practice to create and instantiate components. By calling this method directly when creating the object, as you have done in *Chapter 1*, you are able to pass in your arguments and parameters, giving you the freedom to send through any data that you require, without hardcoding any references.

The pseudo-constructor is useful for remote-access CFCs, a web service, for example. When a remote method is called, ColdFusion creates a new instance of the component, and executes the method requested (and this method only) in the remote call. As such, we would be unable to call an `init()` method at the same time during instantiation, so the ability to set variables within the pseudo-constructor is of great benefit.

Returning values and variables

ColdFusion components allow you to return the values of all allowed data types. The `cfreturn` tag, as we have seen in *Chapter 1*, and in the `getCurrentDate()` method in the `projects.cfc` code, returns a single variable. The return statement in CFScript also returns only one result at a time. If a requirement for the code was to send back more than one variable from the method, a structure or array could be returned containing all required variables and values.

When returning data from a method, you have the ability to explicitly specify what type of value is expected to be returned by using the `returnType` attribute.

returnType

The `returnType` attribute is a required attribute when developing ColdFusion components to be used as web services, but is an optional attribute for all other CFC functions.

This attribute allows you to specify what type of data the value is returning from a method. As it is not a required attribute, if nothing was defined, the default `returnType` would be **'any'**, which allows for all possible eventualities.

However, specifying this attribute will not only enhance the level of detail of the documentation when viewing and reading the code, but will also help to ensure that only the requested data type is returned.

For example, if you wished to return a date, such as in our `getCurrentDate()` method, this attribute would be set to `returnType="date"`.

If your function actually returned a query, or any other data type other than that requested, ColdFusion would display an error with the message, such as "**The value returned from the getCurrentDate() function is not of type query**".

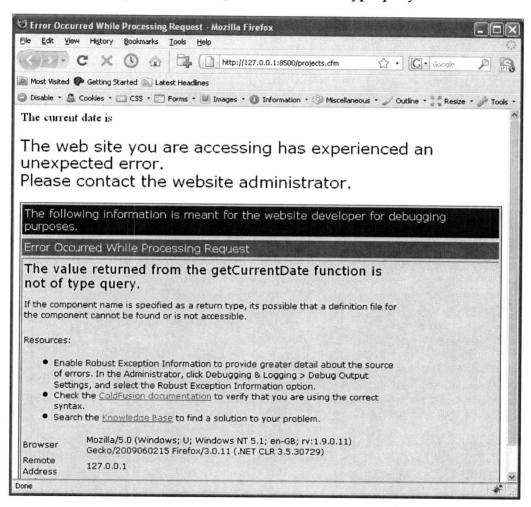

Let's add a new function to our `projects.cfc`. This method will query the `projectTracker` database to return a recordset of all projects currently within the database.

Place the following code beneath the `getCurrentDate()` method:

```
<!--- retrieve all projects within the database --->
<cffunction name="getAllProjects" output="false"
  returnType="query">
  <cfargument name="userID" required="false" type="numeric"
    default="0" />
    <!--- var scope the query variable --->
    <cfset var rstProjects = "" />
    <!--- Wrap the query in try/catch --->
    <cftry>
      <cfquery name="rstProjects" datasource="#This.dsn#">
        SELECT ID, name, status, createdByUserID, dateCreated,
          dateCompleted FROM projects
          <cfif arguments.userID GT 0>
            WHERE createdByUserID = <cfqueryparam cfsqltype="integer"
              value="#arguments.userID#" />
          </cfif>
      </cfquery>
      <!--- catch and display any errors --->
      <cfcatch>
        <cfdump var="#cfcatch#" />
        <cfabort />
      </cfcatch>
    </cftry>
  <cfreturn rstProjects />
</cffunction>
```

Listing 2.4 – Specifying a `returnType` attribute

This method runs a query for all available projects in the database. We are also passing in an optional argument for the UserID, (this is set to 0 by default). If the UserID is sent through and the supplied argument value is greater than the default value, then the WHERE clause within the SQL statement is included in the query.

The query itself has been contained within a `cftry` block to catch any errors. The `cfcatch` tags directly beneath the query will dump the error structure and will stop the function from running to the end.

Taking a look at the opening `cffunction` tag again, you can see the output has been set to `false` to remove any occurrences of whitespace.

```
<cffunction name="getAllProjects" returnType="query" output="false">
</cffunction>
```

Listing 2.5 – Restricting whitespace by using the output attribute

The `returnType` has been set to `query` as we are returning a recordset from the database.

Some of the values available for the `returnType` attribute of `cffunction` are:

- any
- array
- boolean
- numeric
- query
- string
- struct
- xml
- A component name—if the specified type attribute is not one of the previously listed items, ColdFusion will assume that it is a name of a component
- void (no value returned)

 A full list of attributes for the `cfcomponent`, `cffunction`, `cfargument`, and `cfproperty` tags can be found on the Adobe ColdFusion Livedocs reference site: `http://livedocs.adobe.com`.

Access properties

Access attributes control the access to the methods within the component. At its simplest, the access attribute specifies who/what code can access the method and use its services.

Familiarizing yourself with the range of access attributes gives you greater freedom to code remotely using a web service and to integrate other web development tools, such as Flash and Flex, to use ColdFusion output.

It also helps to ensure that you do not restrict function access to a commonly used utility, or open up a method possibly containing private and confidential business logic or code to any third party.

The access attribute is placed within the `cffunction` tag as follows:

```
<cffunction name="getAllProjects" returnType="query" output="false"
  access="public">
</cffunction>
```

Listing 2.6 – Using the `access` attribute

There are four options to choose from when using this attribute, and all four have a different level of access assigned to them.

Private

This is the most restricted access type when it comes to sharing its functionality. The private access ensures that only other functions within the same ColdFusion component are allowed access to the method and its data. This means that no CFML pages, web services, Flash or Flex applications are able to call the method.

Instead, only methods within the same CFC are able to call any private functions. Any attempts to access the private function from an external source (anywhere but within the CFC) will result in an error message to the user stating that the function could not be found. Although it is written in your code, due to its private access restrictions, it will not be identified.

To call a private function from another method within the same ColdFusion component, you would use code similar to this example:

```
<cffunction name="baseNumber" returnType="numeric" access="private">
  <cfargument name="a" type="numeric" required="true" />
    <cfset Var x = arguments.a />
  <cfreturn x />
</cffunction>
<cffunction name="multiplyNumbers" returntype="string">
  <cfargument name="a" type="numeric" required="true" />
  <cfargument name="b" type="numeric" required="true" />
    <cfset Var x = 10 />
    <cfset y = baseNumber(a) />
  <cfreturn y & " multiplied by " & x & " = " & x * arguments.b />
</cffunction>
```

Listing 2.7 – Calling a method within from within another

In our multiplication methods shown in *Chapter 1*, our `multiplyNumbers()` method calls the `baseNumber()` method within the same component.

As this method is a utility function that does not return any data required for anything other than functions within the same CFC, we do not want or need the `baseNumber()` function to be externally accessible, so here we have set the access attribute to `private`.

Package

The Package access option can be invoked only by other functions in the same component or by another component within the same package. This is a step up from the Private option as it not only allows the 'parent' component to read the method, but also opens up the method to other components.

A package is simply a directory containing CFC files, created and structured to store relevant groups of components that share a common purpose or resources for a task, mentioned in *Chapter 1*.

Public

The Public access option is the default access role for any CFC method if one hasn't been declared. This option allows any CFML code and other components within the application, access to the function and its services.

Remote

The Remote option is the most open access available to your CFC methods. It allows the function to be accessible by anyone and everything. It can be used from within the same component, from other components (whether they are in the same package or not), any CFML page on your server, Flash and Flex remoting services, web service clients, or any HTTP requests.

Getting information about your CFC

ColdFusion components have the unique ability to look within themselves and display information regarding their content. It can display all of the methods contained within the component, all of the properties within the functions, including parameters and arguments, and what, if any, information is to be returned. This is commonly referred to as **introspection**.

Introspection

Introspection provides a valuable tool for gaining a comprehensive snapshot of your code.

This is particularly useful when working in a larger team environment and sharing code that may have been written by another developer, or perhaps in those rare moments when you forget what functions you have written in a CFC within your extensive component library.

CFC Explorer

One method to obtain information about the CFC contents is to view the component directly in your web browser. ColdFusion has a built-in CFC Explorer tool that is able to read a ColdFusion component and display its data directly to the end user.

When directly accessing the CFC in your browser, you will be sent to the ColdFusion administrator screen, where you may be prompted to enter your login details if you have any set, which is to ensure that only authorized administrators are able to view the component and its properties.

Using your web browser, go to the following address to view the `projects.cfc`:

`http://localhost:8500/com/Projects/projects.cfc`.

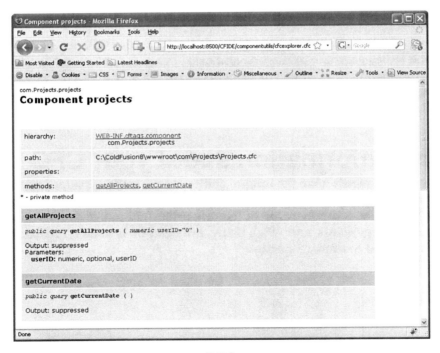

This method of introspection provides a clear and detailed visual reference of the component and its included methods, but the level of detail returned depends heavily on the amount of detail and attributes you choose to include when developing the component.

Component Doc

ColdFusion also includes an application that reads all of the components on your server, and allows you to inspect and view whichever component you choose to. The application clearly and neatly displays your CFC library in a multiple-framed format, which is easy to navigate and read.

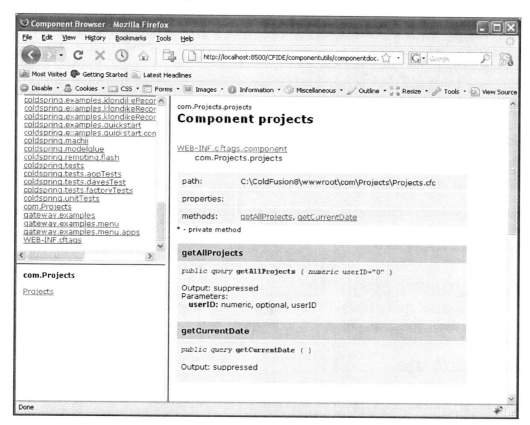

This is also accessible through your web browser by going to the following address: `http://localhost:8500/CFIDE/componentutils/componentdoc.cfm`.

Document your code

Having these resources available to you is a great help but of no major use unless your code is well-formed, well-documented, and commented wherever possible.

As a developer, you may or may not comment your code. It may depend on your working environment (if you work alone or in a team, however large or small), your coding practices and standards (you may be detailed when it comes to writing comments, or you may not even bother to write any) as well as time restrictions on a project where you may be against the clock to publish your application, and sometimes plain forgetfulness.

Benefits of documentation

By ensuring that your code is well-documented using some of the standard tag attributes within the CFC, you can greatly enhance the longevity and usefulness of your component and declare important information on its usage and requirements.

This is particularly useful when working in a team environment where you may be reading a CFC written by another developer, or someone reading a component written by you, and all information relating to the component, the functions, and arguments required are clearly documented and understandable.

This helps to alleviate any confusion over requirements and the purpose of the code.

The `cfcomponent`, `cffunction`, `cfargument`, and `cfproperty` tags all accept two very important (although optional) attributes, which are ideal for creating well-documented components.

Displayname attribute

The `displayname` attribute allows you to provide a more focused, descriptive name for a component, function, argument, or property tag.

Hint attribute

The `hint` attribute can be used for specifying a bit more detail about the component, function, argument, or property to which it has been assigned.

Let's amend our `projects.cfc` file, and add the `displayname` and `hint` attributes to specify more information:

```
<cfcomponent name="Projects" output="false"
  displayname="A CFC called 'Projects'"
  hint="Used to access project related functions">
```

Listing 2.8 – Provide more details using attributes

An ideal place to use the `hint` attribute is within the `cfargument` tag. The name given to the argument may make sense to the developer who has written the function, but may be a little confusing or vague for any other developers looking at the code within the component.

By adding the `hint` attribute to the `cfargument` tag, you are able to specify a description of what the argument is, and what is expected or required to be sent in to it, instantly providing a helpful reference for others within your team, or as a reminder for when you revisit the code a few months later.

Description attribute

Another optional attribute that can be used within the `cffunction` tag is the `description` attribute, which allows you provide a short text description explaining the purpose of the method.

```
<cffunction name="getCurrentDate" access="public"
  output="false" returnType="date"
  description="I return the current date as dd/mm/yyyy">
  <cfreturn dateFormat(Now(), "dd/mm/yyyy") />
</cffunction>
```

Listing 2.9 – Setting the `description` attribute

Although this attribute will not be displayed when using introspection, a good practice would be to include it in all functions that you write and develop, purely to act as a useful reminder to anyone reading the code.

User-defined metadata

ColdFusion components provide you with the ability to define custom metadata information as attributes, which can be applied to the `cfcomponent`, `cffunction`, `cfargument`, and `cfproperty` tags.

Although these will not have any direct effect on the functionality of the tags or the CFC as a whole, they do allow you to enhance your component documentation by providing more information.

Creating a metadata attribute is a simple case of providing a name/value pair for the information you wish to include.

When defining and naming custom metadata attributes, you are not allowed to use a name reserved by any existing ColdFusion component, cffunction, cfargument, or cfproperty tag.

In the following example, we are creating additional custom attributes to an opening cfcomponent tag to specify the name of the application that uses the component, and the name of the developer who wrote the CFC:

```
<cfcomponent name="Projects" output="false"
   displayname="A CFC called 'Projects'"
   hint="Used to access project related functions"
   Application="Project Tracker" Developer="Matt James">
```

Listing 2.10 – Defining custom attributes

Obtaining CFC metadata

Metadata attributes have no impact when instantiating the component or object, and as a result do not hinder the processing time taken to create them. They are incredibly useful functions, which can be used to view not only user-defined metadata but all metadata attributed to the component, and can be a quick and efficient way of viewing key information relating to the object you wish to view.

Unlike the other documentation methods available to you, they will not be visible when viewing the component through introspection.

To obtain this information from your CFCs, ColdFusion has two functions to retrieve metadata: getMetaData() and getComponentMetaData().

getMetaData

This function can be used to retrieve metadata attributes and information for any component instance, once it has been instantiated or created. The function accepts one parameter, which is the expression of the object you wish it to inspect.

For example, amend the following projects.cfm file to display the information from the previously created objProjects object:

```
<cfscript>
  objProjects = createObject("component", "com.Projects.Projects");
  objProjectsMeta = getMetaData(objProjects);
</cfscript>
<cfdump var="#objProjectsMeta#" />
```

Listing 2.11 – Obtaining metadata from the component

The output returned from the getMetaData() function is a structure that contains detailed information from the component. This includes an array of all functions written within the component, their method and argument attributes, as well as all metadata from the core CFC (such as displayname, hint, file path, and output), including any user-defined attributes that may have been added.

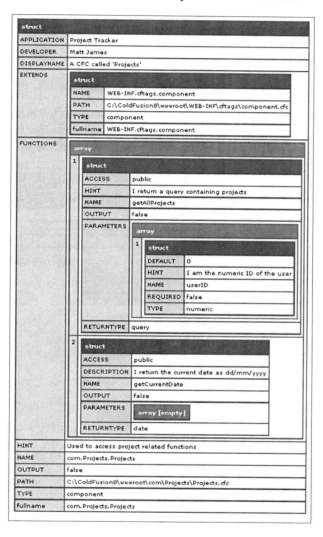

getComponentMetaData

The getComponentMetaData() function produces exactly the same results, but can be used to obtain the information from any component, whether instantiated or not.

This function accepts one single parameter, which is the path to the component you wish to inspect and retrieve information for.

```
<cfscript>
  objContactsMeta = getComponentMetaData('com.contacts.contacts');
</cfscript>
<cfdump var="#objContactsMeta#" />
```

Listing 2.12 – Details using getComponentMetaData function

Here, we are using the getComponentMetaData() function to retrieve and dump the output from a component that has not been instantiated. The parameter has been provided as the dot notation path to the component we wish to introspect.

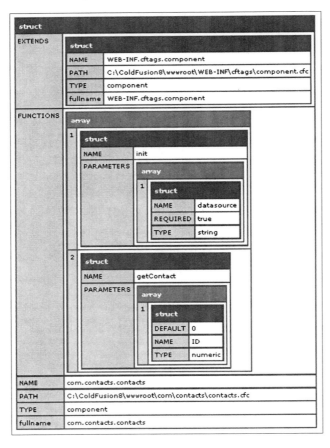

You can see that the output from the `getComponentMetaData()` function displays the same **struct** of arrays as the `getMetaData()` method.

 Custom attributes should contain strings only. You cannot set metadata using ColdFusion expressions or variables.

Returning metadata

The metadata functions provide an instantly visual detailed breakdown of a component's attributes and properties. As well as being a valuable resource for documentation, the custom attributes are also accessible and can be used in your ColdFusion template pages. Amend your `projects.cfm` file as follows:

```
<cfscript>
  objProjectsMeta = getMetaData(objProjects);
</cfscript>
<cfoutput>
  Component: #objProjectsMeta.Name#<br />
  Written by: #objProjectsMeta.Developer#<br />
  Application: #objProjectsMeta.Application#
</cfoutput>
```

Listing 2.13 – Displaying metadata

Here, we are referencing the name of the attributes we wish to display. Notice that you can extract not only custom metadata, but standard CFC attributes from the component.

The output from the previous code is as follows:

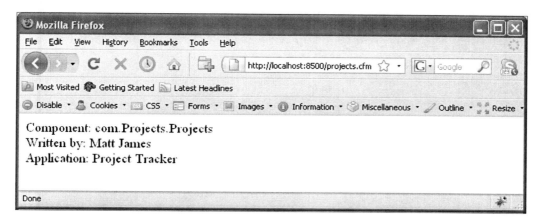

In essence, as well as providing detailed structural information on the object or component, using either the `getMetaData()` or `getComponentMetaData()` functions in this way will allow you to write your own ColdFusion pages to deal with introspection, should you wish to do so.

Detailed introspection

From the minimal effort of adding extra `hint` and `displayname` tags, the output generated by the CFC Explorer tool for introspection has been enhanced to display much more detail pertaining to the component and its properties.

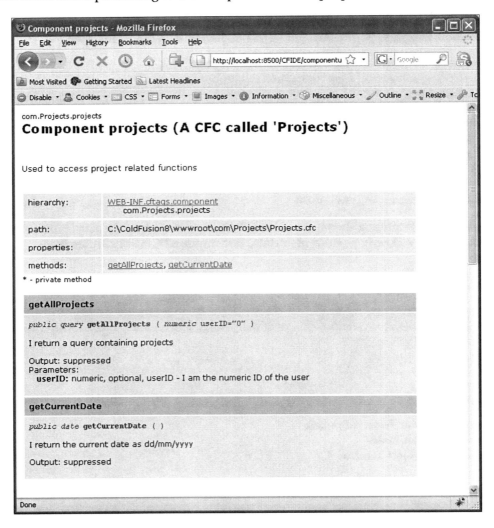

In a shared working environment, this would be of great benefit to all developers wishing to collaborate on a project and the CFC resources used within.

Summary

In this chapter, we have discussed the benefits of including additional attributes to your components and their included properties and methods to improve on documentation.

Other topics that we have covered in this chapter are:

- Using the pseudo-constructor to create variables
- Whitespace suppression using the output attribute
- Returning variables from your functions

3

Building Your First Bean

Following the code and examples included in the previous two chapters, we now have a fairly good understanding of what a ColdFusion component is, how to write one, how to create an object, and how to use the methods included within the CFC.

Object-oriented programming is a form of programming paradigm that utilizes "objects", structures of data that consist of data fields and methods, and the object interactions for development.

Focusing on data rather than processes, the OOP methodology uses self-sufficient modules (the objects), which contain all the information they require to manipulate their own data structure.

In this chapter, we will look at the first ColdFusion component within the **OOP design pattern**, the Bean.

We will also cover the following topics:

- What is a Bean?
- The benefits of using a Bean
- The requirements for a Bean
- Setting and retrieving values from the Object

What is a Bean?

Although the terminology evokes the initial reaction of cooking ingredients or a tin of food from a supermarket, the Bean is an incredibly important piece of the object-oriented design pattern.

The term 'Bean' originates from the Java programming language, and for those developers out there who enjoy their coffee as much as I do, the thought process behind it will make sense: **Java = Coffee = Coffee Bean = Bean**.

A Bean is basically the building block for your object. Think of it as a blueprint for the information you want each object to hold and contain. In relation to other ColdFusion components, the Bean is a relatively simple CFC that primarily has two roles in life:

- to store information or a collection of values
- to return the information or collection of values when required

But what is it really?

Typically, a ColdFusion bean is a single CFC built to encapsulate and store a single record of data, and not a recordset query result, which would normally hold more than one record. This is not to say that the information within the Bean should only be pulled from one record within a database table, or that the data needs to be only a single string — far from it.

You can include information in your Bean from any source at your disposal; however, the Bean can only ever contain one set of information.

Your Bean represents a specific entity. This entity could be a person, a car, or a building. Essentially, any 'single' object can be represented by a bean in terms of development.

The Bean holds information about the entity it is written for. Imagine we have a Bean to represent a person, and this Bean will hold details on that individual's name, age, hair color, and so on. These details are the properties for the entity, and together they make up the completed Bean for that person.

In reality, the idea of the Bean itself is incredibly similar to a structure. You could easily represent the person entity in the form of a structure, as follows:

```
<!---Build an empty structure to emulate a Person entity.--->
<cfset stuPerson = {
  name = '', age = '',
  hairColor = ''} />
```

Listing: 3.1 – Creating an entity structure

This seems like an entirely feasible way to hold your data, right? To some extent it is. You have a structure, complete with properties for the object/entity, wrapped up into one tidy package.

You can easily update the structure to hold the properties for the individual, and retrieve the information for each property, as seen in the following code example:

```
<!---Build an empty structure to emulate a Person entity.--->
<cfset stuPerson = {
  name = '', age = '',
  hairColor = ''} />
<cfdump var="#stuPerson#" label="Person - empty data" />
<!---Update the structure with data and display the output--->
<cfset StructUpdate(
  stuPerson, 'name', 'Matt Gifford') />
<cfset StructUpdate(
  stuPerson, 'hairColor', 'Brown') />
<br />
<cfdump var="#stuPerson#" label="Person - data added" />
<br />
<cfoutput>
  Name: #stuPerson.name#<br />
  Hair: #stuPerson.hairColor#
</cfoutput>
```

Listing 3.2 – Populating the entity structure

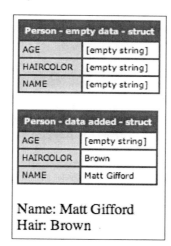

Although the structure is an incredibly simple method of retaining and accessing data, particularly when looking at the code, they do not suit the purpose of a blueprint for an entity very well, and as soon as you have populated the structure it is no longer a blueprint, but a specific entity.

Imagine that you were reading data from the database and wanted to use the structure for every person who was drawn out from the query. Sure enough, you could create a standard structure that was persistent in the Application scope, for example. You could then loop through the query and populate the structure with the recordset results. For every person object you wanted, you could run ColdFusion's built-in Duplicate() function to create a copy of the original 'base' structure, and apply it to a new variable.

Or perhaps, the structure might need to be written again on every page it is required in, or maybe written on a separate .cfm page that is included into the template using cfinclude.

Perhaps over time, your application will grow, requirements will change, and extra details will need to be stored. You would then be faced with the task of changing and updating every instance of the structures across your entire application to include additional keys and values, or remove some from the structure.

This route could possibly have you searching for code, testing, and debugging at every turn, and would not be the best method to optimize your development time and to enhance the scalability of your application.

Taking the time to invest in your code base and development practices from the start will greatly enhance your application, development time, and go some way to reduce unnecessary headaches caused by spaghetti code and lack of structure.

The benefit of using beans

By creating a Bean for each entity within your application, you have created a specific blueprint for the data we wish to hold for that entity. The rules of encapsulation are adhered to, and nothing is hardcoded into our CFC.

We have already seen how our objects are created, and how we can pass variables and data into them, which can be through the init() method during instantiation or perhaps as an argument when calling an included function within the component.

Every time you need to use the blueprint for the Person class, you can simply create an instance of the Bean.

You instantly have a completely fresh new object ready to populate with specific properties, and you can create a fully populated Person object in just one line of code within your application.

The main purpose of a Bean in object-oriented development is to capture and encapsulate a variety of different objects, be they structures, arrays, queries, or strings for example, into one single object, which is the Bean itself.

The Bean can then be passed around your application where required, containing all of the included information, instead of the application itself sending the many individual objects around or storing each one in, for example, the Application or Session scope, which could get messy.

This creates a nicely packaged container that holds all of the information we need to send and use within our applications, and acts as a much easier way to manage the data we are passing around.

If your blueprints need updating, for example more properties need to be added to the objects, you only have one file to modify, the CFC of the Bean itself. This instantly removes the problematic issues of having to search for every instance or every structure for your object throughout your entire code base.

A Bean essentially provides you with a consistent and elegant interface, which will help you to organize your data into objects, removing the need to create, persist, and replicate ad-hoc structures.

Creating our first Bean

Let's look at creating a Bean for use with the projects table in the database. We'll continue with the Person Bean as the primary example, and create the CFC to handle person objects.

An introduction to UML

Before we start coding the component, let's have a quick look at a visual representation of the object using Unified Modeling Language (UML).

UML is a widely-used method to display, share, and reference objects, Classes, workflows, and structures in the world of object-oriented programming, which you will come into contact with during your time with OOP development.

The modeling language itself is incredibly detailed and in-depth, and can express such a wide array of details and information.

Person object in UML

In this example, let's take a look at the basics of UML and the visual representation of the Person component that we will create, which looks like this:

Person
-firstName:string
-lastName:string
-gender:string
-dateofbirth:string
-hairColor:string
+init(firstName lastName gender dateofbirth hairColor):Person
+setFirstName(firstName)
+getFirstName():string
+setLastName(lastName)
+getLastName():string
+setGender(gender)
+getGender():string
+setDateOfBirth(dateofbirth)
+getDateOfBirth():string
+setHairColor(hairColor)
+getHairColor():string

At first glances, you can instantly see what variables and functions our component consists of.

With most UML objects, it is broken into segments for easier digestion. The actual name of the component is clearly visible within the top section of the diagram.

In the second section, we include the variables that will be included within our object. These have a '-' character in front of them, to indicate that these variables are private and are hidden within the component (they are not accessible externally). These variables are followed by the variable type, separated by a colon (':'). This lets you easily see which variable type is expected. In this example, we can see that all of the variables are strings.

In the bottom section of the diagram we include the function references, which contain all methods within the component.

All of the functions are prefixed with a '+' to indicate that they are publically accessible, and so are available to be called externally from the component itself.

For any functions that require parameters, they are included inside the parenthesis. If a function returns a value, the `returnType` is specified after the ':'.

Based upon this UML diagram, let's create the core wrapper for the CFC, and create the constructor method — the `init()` function.

Create a new file called `Person.cfc` and save this file in the following location within your project folder: `com/packtApp/oop/beans`.

```
<cfcomponent displayname="Person" output="false"
  hint="I am the Person Class.">
  <cfproperty name="firstName" type="string" default="" />
  <cfproperty name="lastName" type="string" default="" />
  <cfproperty name="gender" type="string" default="" />
  <cfproperty name="dateofbirth" type="string" default="" />
  <cfproperty name="hairColor" type="string" default="" />

  <!--- Pseudo-constructor --->
  <cfset variables.instance = {
    firstName = '', lastName = '', gender= '',
    dateofbirth = '', hairColor = ''
  } />
  <cffunction name="init" access="public" output="false"
    returntype="any" hint="I am the constructor method for the Person
    Class.">
    <cfargument name="firstName" required="true"
      type="String" default="" hint="I am the first name." />
    <cfargument name="lastName" required="true"
      type="String" default="" hint="I am the last name." />
    <cfargument name="gender" required="true"
      type="String" default="" hint="I am the gender." />
    <cfargument name="dateofbirth" required="true"
      type="String" default="" hint="I am the date of birth." />
```

```
    <cfargument name="hairColor" required="true"
      type="String" default="" hint="I am the hair color." />
    <cfreturn this />
  </cffunction>
</cfcomponent>
```

Listing 3.3 - `com/packtApp/oop/beans/Person.cfc`

Here, we have the `init()` method for the `Person.cfc` and the arguments defined for each property within the object. The bean will hold the values of its properties within the `variables.instance` structure, which we have defined above the `init()` method as a pseudo-constructor.

What makes a Bean a Bean

We know that a Bean is a CFC representing a specific entity. But what differentiates a Bean from a normal ColdFusion component?

There are two conventions that a CFC can follow in order to officially declare it as a Bean, which are:

- The class must have a public default/no-argument constructor
- The class properties must be accessible to allow easy inspection and updating of Bean state

A default/no-argument constructor

Looking at the code we have just written, we can see the constructor method has the arguments required to populate the project Bean entity. However, when we instantiate the Bean in our code, we may not yet have that information to hand and we may not know what values to pass into the object to populate the properties.

As such, we have set the `required` attribute for each argument to `required="false"`, and have set a default value for each argument based upon its expected type. For example, all arguments expecting a string have a blank default value, and all arguments expecting a numeric value have their default value set to "0".

So, although the constructor method does have arguments, they are not required to be populated upon creation, making this method a 'no-argument constructor', which conforms to the first requirement for Beans.

Easily accessible for introspection

Once the object has been instantiated using the `init()` method, a structure variable called "instance" is created within the `Variables` scope of the CFC. As we have discovered in *Chapter 1*, the `Variables` scope is a local private scope within the component, and cannot be modified from anywhere except within the CFC itself.

The `variables.instance` structure will hold data for the Bean's properties, and in order to access the structure to write data and read values from the Bean we need two methods for each property within the CFC.

Methods used to write values to properties are commonly referred to as **Setters** or **Mutators**, while methods used to retrieve values from the Bean are known as **Getters** or **Accessors**.

Setters/Mutators

Let's add some setter methods to our `Person.cfc` so that we can set values within the object. The methods should be placed underneath the `init()` method.

```
<!--- setters /mutators --->
<cffunction name="setFirstName" access="public"
  output="false" hint="I set the first name into the
  variables.instance scope.">
  <cfargument name="firstName" required="true"
    type="String" hint="I am the person's firstName." />
    <cfset variables.instance.firstName = arguments.firstName />
</cffunction>

<cffunction name="setLastName" access="private"
  output="false" hint="I set the last name into the
  variables.instance scope.">
  <cfargument name="lastName" required="true"
    type="String" hint="I am the person's lastName." />
    <cfset variables.instance.lastName = arguments.lastName />
</cffunction>
```

Listing 3.4 – Adding mutators to `Person.cfc`

The typical naming convention for a setter method is to call the function **set[Property]**, replacing [property] with the name of the property within the Bean you wish to set. In the previous example, we have defined the `setFirstName()` and `setLastName()` functions.

Each function takes one argument, which is the value we want to set the specific property to, and the arguments are all set to `required="true"` to ensure we pass through the values when mutating the Bean.

When you call `setFirstName(x)` from within the `init()` method, which we will see in a later code example, the function will assign the value sent through in the argument to the `firstName` key within the `variables.instance` scope.

The setter functions do not return any information. They are purely used for setting information, not for reading and supplying back to the user.

Getters/Accessors

Now we have the methods in place to set values within the project Bean, but we also need to retrieve the information for each specific property, and we do so by creating one getter method within our CFC for each property. Place these methods underneath the setter methods defined in your CFC:

```
<!--- getters / accessors --->
<cffunction name="getFirstName" access="public"
  output="false" hint="I return the first name.">
  <cfreturn variables.instance.firstName />
</cffunction>

<cffunction name="getLastName" access="public"
  output="false" hint="I return the last name.">
  <cfreturn variables.instance.lastName />
</cffunction>
```

Listing 3.5 – Adding accessors to `Person.cfc`

Simple and elegant in terms of code and function, the getter methods also follow the same naming convention as the setter functions, so in the previous example we have `getFirstName()` and `getLastName()` to retrieve the values for those specific Bean properties.

The getter (or accessor) methods take no arguments. Instead, they simply read the specific key from the `variables.instance` structure and return that data back to the user.

We now have an easy way to interact, amend, and retrieve the properties within the Bean itself, thanks to the getter and setter methods we have defined. The CFC now conforms to the second requirement for true Bean status.

Completing our Projects Bean

In our current code for the Person Bean, we have the two methods for getting and setting the `firstName` and `lastName` properties. The CFC needs to set the values of the properties upon instantiation, so we need to amend the `init()` method like so:

```
<cffunction name="init" access="public" output="false"
  returntype="any" hint="I am the constructor method for the Person
  Class.">
  <cfargument name="firstName" required="true" type="String"
    default="" hint="I am the first name." />
  <cfargument name="lastName" required="true" type="String"
    default="" hint="I am the last name." />
  <cfargument name="gender" required="true" type="String"
    default="" hint="I am the gender." />
  <cfargument name="dateofbirth" required="true" type="String"
    default="" hint="I am the date of birth." />
  <cfargument name="hairColor" required="true" type="String"
    default="" hint="I am the hair color." />
  <!--- Set the initial values of the Bean --->
  <cfscript>
    setFirstName(arguments.firstName);
    setLastName(arguments.lastName);
  </cfscript>
  <cfreturn this />
</cffunction>
```

Listing 3.6 – Setting the variables within the constructor

You can see that we have placed the setFirstName() and setLastName() methods
into the constructor function. These will set the relevant variables.instance
properties with the values sent in through the arguments, which will use the default
values if no arguments are specified.

Now, let's add the rest of the getter and setter methods to the CFC to complete the
Bean, which should look like this:

```
<cfcomponent displayname="Person" output="false"
  hint="I am the Person Class.">
  <cfproperty name="firstName" type="string" default="" />
  <cfproperty name="lastName" type="string" default="" />
  <cfproperty name="gender" type="string" default="" />
  <cfproperty name="dateofbirth" type="string" default="" />
  <cfproperty name="hairColor" type="string" default="" />

  <!--- Pseudo-constructor --->
  <cfset variables.instance = {
    firstName = '', lastName = '', gender = '',
    dateofbirth = '', hairColor = ''
  } />

  <cffunction name="init" access="public" output="false"
```

```
returntype="any" hint="I am the constructor method for the Person
Class.">
  <cfargument name="firstName" required="true" type="String"
    default="" hint="I am the first name." />
  <cfargument name="lastName" required="true" type="String"
    default="" hint="I am the last name." />
  <cfargument name="gender" required="true" type="String"
    default="" hint="I am the gender." />
  <cfargument name="dateofbirth" required="true" type="String"
    default="" hint="I am the date of birth." />
  <cfargument name="hairColor" required="true" type="String"
    default="" hint="I am the hair color." />
    <!--- Set the initial values of the Bean --->
    <cfscript>
      setFirstName(arguments.firstName);
      setLastName(arguments.lastName);
      setGender(arguments.gender);
      setDateOfBirth(arguments.dateofbirth);
      setHairColor(arguments.hairColor);
    </cfscript>
  <cfreturn this />
</cffunction>

<!--- getters / accessors --->
<cffunction name="getFirstName" access="public"
  output="false" hint="I return the first name.">
  <cfreturn variables.instance.firstName />
</cffunction>

<cffunction name="getLastName" access="public"
  output="false" hint="I return the last name.">
  <cfreturn variables.instance.lastName />
</cffunction>

<cffunction name="getGender" access="public"
  output="false" hint="I return the gender.">
  <cfreturn variables.instance.gender />
</cffunction>

<cffunction name="getDateOfBirth" access="public"
  output="false" hint="I return the date of birth.">
  <cfreturn variables.instance.dateofbirth />
</cffunction>

<cffunction name="getHairColor" access="public"
```

```
    output="false" hint="I return the hair color.">
      <cfreturn variables.instance.hairColor />
    </cffunction>


    <!--- setters /mutators --->
    <cffunction name="setFirstName" access="public"
      output="false" hint="I set the first name into the
      variables.instance scope.">
      <cfargument name="firstName" required="true"
        type="String" hint="I am the person's firstName." />
        <cfset variables.instance.firstName = arguments.firstName />
    </cffunction>


    <cffunction name="setLastName" access="public"
      output="false" hint="I set the last name into the
      variables.instance scope.">
      <cfargument name="lastName" required="true"
        type="String" hint="I am the person's lastName." />
        <cfset variables.instance.lastName = arguments.lastName />
    </cffunction>


    <cffunction name="setGender" access="public"
      output="false" hint="I set the gender into the
      variables.instance scope.">
      <cfargument name="gender" required="true"
        type="String" hint="I am the person's gender." />
        <cfset variables.instance.gender = arguments.gender />
    </cffunction>


    <cffunction name="setDateOfBirth" access="public"
      output="false" hint="I set the dateofbirth into the
      variables.instance scope.">
      <cfargument name="dateofbirth" required="true"
        type="String" hint="I am the person's dateofbirth." />
        <cfset variables.instance.dateofbirth =
          arguments.dateofbirth />
    </cffunction>


    <cffunction name="setHairColor" access="public"
      output="false" hint="I set the hairColor into the
      variables.instance scope.">
      <cfargument name="hairColor" required="true"
        type="String" hint="I am the person's hairColor." />
        <cfset variables.instance.hairColor = arguments.hairColor />
    </cffunction>
</cfcomponent>
```

Listing 3.7 – A complete `Person.cfc`

Listing 3.7 contains a complete Person component. All properties now have a getter and setter method. We have also added all required setter methods into the constructor to set variables upon instantiation.

It may not look as clean and tidy as the project structure code we had looked at previously in this chapter, but the Bean is properly encapsulated and will allow you to easily update and get your data from the object with minimal fuss, and any future updates required for the object will only need to be written in one place—the Person CFC itself.

Calling our project Bean

We have already ensured that our Bean matches one of the conventions and that it is a no-argument constructor. We can create the object without sending any arguments to the `init()` method, as follows:

```
<cfscript>
  // Instantiate the Person object
  objPerson = createObject('component',
    'com.packtApp.oop.beans.Person').init();
</cfscript>
```

Listing 3.8 – Instantiating the object

With the Person Bean now created, we can send data into the object.

As the values are being stored in the `Variables` scope within the CFC, we have no way of accessing this scope directly from outside of the component. To make life a little easier when it comes to debugging the values stored in the `variables.instances` structure, let's add the following method to the end of our `Person.cfc` file, before the closing `</cfcomponent>` tag:

```
<!--- utils --->
<cffunction name="getMemento" access="public"
  output="false" hint="I return a dumped struct of the
  variables.instance scope.">
  <cfreturn variables.instance />
</cffunction>
```

Listing 3.9 – `getMemento()` method for `Person.cfc`

This `getMemento()` method will give us the ability to output the `variables.instance` structure onto our `.cfm` template so that we can see the values currently stored within it.

We can use the function as the one shown in the following example, which will provide us with a visual output of the current values within the Bean:

```
<cfscript>
  // Instantiate the Person object
  objPerson = createObject('component',
    'com.packtApp.oop.beans.Person').init();
</cfscript>
<!--- View the content of the variables.instance scope using the
  getMemento() method--->
<cfdump var="#objPerson.getMemento()#" label="Person -
  variables.instance" />
```

Listing 3.10 – Viewing the `variables.instance` data

Person - variables.instance - struct	
DATEOFBIRTH	[empty string]
FIRSTNAME	[empty string]
GENDER	[empty string]
HAIRCOLOR	[empty string]
LASTNAME	[empty string]

The returned output from the `getMemento()` method shows us that, as we already knew, the properties within the object are as of yet unpopulated and simply hold the default values as defined in the constructor method.

Populating the Bean

Beans are wonderful things. They can be populated by data in the FORM or URL scopes, or from data drawn from a query recordset. We will be exploring these options later in the book when we look into more code examples.

For now, let's populate some of the properties using the setter functions we have written.

Copy the following code to pass variables into the properties within the Bean, and we'll run the `getMemento()` method one more time to test the results:

```
<cfscript>
  // Instantiate the Person object
  objPerson = createObject('component',
    'com.packtApp.oop.beans.Person').init();
</cfscript>
```

```
<!---View the content of the variables.instance scope using the
  getMemento() method--->
<cfdump var="#objPerson.getMemento()#"label="Person -
  variables.instance" />
<cfscript>
  objPerson.setFirstName('Gary');
  objPerson.setLastName('Brown');
  objPerson.setGender('Male');
  objPerson.setHairColor('Brown');
  objPerson.setDateOfBirth('01/04/1979');
</cfscript>
<!---View the content of the variables.instance scope using the
  getMemento() method--->
<cfdump var="#objPerson.getMemento()#" label="Person -
  populated variables.instance" />
```

Listing 3.11 – Populating the Person object

Person - variables.instance - struct	
DATEOFBIRTH	[empty string]
FIRSTNAME	[empty string]
GENDER	[empty string]
HAIRCOLOR	[empty string]
LASTNAME	[empty string]

Person - populated variables.instance - struct	
DATEOFBIRTH	01/04/1979
FIRSTNAME	Gary
GENDER	Male
HAIRCOLOR	Brown
LASTNAME	Brown

From the output in the second structure, you can see that the values have successfully been inserted into the variables.instance structure.

Read/Write Bean

The types of Bean we have written in this chapter's code examples are also thought of as **read/write Beans**.

A read/write Bean has the setter/mutator methods set to **public**. Our Person object UML diagram had every function set to public access, which was visible by the '+' before each function name. This means that a value of any property within the object can be changed outside of the init() method.

For example, once we have instantiated our object on our `.cfm` template page, we can change property values as we need to, like so:

```
<cfscript>
  // Instantiate the Person object
  objPerson = createObject('component',
    'com.packtApp.oop.beans.Person').init();
</cfscript>
<!---View the content of the variables.instance scope using the
  getMemento() method--->
<cfscript>
  objPerson.setFirstName('Matt');
  objPerson.setLastName('Tubbs');
  objPerson.setGender('Male');
  objPerson.setHairColor('Brown');
  objPerson.setDateOfBirth('01/04/1979');
</cfscript>
<cfdump var="#objPerson.getMemento()#" label="Person -
  populated variables.instance" />
<cfscript>
  objPerson.setFirstName('James');
  objPerson.setLastName('Crockett');
  objPerson.setGender('Male');
  objPerson.setHairColor('Blonde');
  objPerson.setDateOfBirth('29/02/1964');
</cfscript>
<!---View the content of the variables.instance scope using the
  getMemento() method--->
<cfdump var="#objPerson.getMemento()#" label="Person -
  amended variables.instance" />
```

Listing 3.12 – Populating the read-write Bean

In this code listing, we have instantiated our Bean object, inserted some data using the set methods, and dumped the value of the `variables.instance` scope onto the page.

We then call the setter methods once more to assign values to those properties within the object, and run the dump method again to view the updated properties, the output of which is shown as follows:

Person - populated variables.instance - struct	
DATEOFBIRTH	01/04/1979
FIRSTNAME	Matt
GENDER	Male
HAIRCOLOR	Brown
LASTNAME	Tubbs
Person - amended variables.instance - struct	
DATEOFBIRTH	29/02/1964
FIRSTNAME	James
GENDER	Male
HAIRCOLOR	Blonde
LASTNAME	Crockett

Read-only Bean

An alternative Bean type is the **read-only Bean**. This differs from the read/write Bean as no setter/mutator method can be called directly from any external page.

This is achieved by setting the `access` attribute for the setter methods to `private`, as follows:

```
<cffunction name="setFirstName" access="private" output="false"
  hint="I set the first name into the variables.instance scope.">
  <cfargument name="firstName" required="true" type="String"
  hint="I am the person's firstName." />
    <cfset variables.instance.firstName = arguments.firstName />
</cffunction>
```

Listing 3.13 – Amending a set method to private access

If we ran the same code in our previous example, we would receive the following error on screen:

The following information is meant for the website developer for debugging purposes.
Error Occurred While Processing Request
The method setFirstName was not found in component /Applications/ColdFusion9/wwwroot/OOP/com/packtApp/oop/beans/Person.cfc.

Ensure that the method is defined, and that it is spelled correctly.

The error occurred in **/Applications/ColdFusion9/wwwroot/OOP/index.cfm: line 22**

```
20 :
21 : <cfscript>
22 :     objPerson.setFirstName('Matt');
23 :     objPerson.setLastName('Tubbs');
24 :     objPerson.setGender('Male');
```

By setting the `access` attribute on the setter methods to `private`, the only way to alter the values of the object's properties is to send argument values through the component's `init()` constructor method:

```
<cfscript>
  // Instantiate the Person object
  objPerson = createObject('component',
    'com.packtApp.oop.beans.Person').init(
    firstName='Matt', lastName='James', gender='Male',
    hairColor='Brown', dateofbirth='01/04/1979'
  );
</cfscript>
<!---View the content of the variables.instance scope using the
  getMemento() method--->
<cfdump var="#objPerson.getMemento()#" label="Person -
  populated variables.instance" />
```

Listing 3.14 – Populating the read-only `Person.cfc`

The code within the `cfscript` block is almost identical to the previous example. The main difference is the way the data is being sent into the object.

Here, you can see that the values are being sent in through the `init()` method as name/value pairs. The values are then passed to the arguments within the constructor method and the setter/mutator functions update the properties within the `variables.instance` structure.

The getter/accessor functions remain as `access="public"` as we need to be able to access those methods and retrieve values from the object on any external page or process for use in our application.

Helpful objects

In our current Person object we simply return the variables as they currently exist within the object.

Your components do not have to simply be static in that respect, and can easily perform work for you using the data it currently holds. This could include mathematical calculations, recordset queries, or string concatenations using the existing information.

Let's customize our `Person.cfc` and include some new methods that will enhance the object and allow us to obtain more information from the Bean.

We already hold the first and last name values within the component, and we can access these individually using the getFirstName() and getLastName() methods respectively.

Let's create a method to return the complete full name of the person by concatenating the string values within a new method.

We also have access to the dateofbirth variable. Let's also add a new method that will calculate the person's current age in years.

Listing 3.15 now shows the revised complete Person.cfc, which includes two helper methods:

```
<cfcomponent displayname="Person" output="false"
  hint="I am the Person Class.">
  <cfproperty name="firstName" type="string" default="" />
  <cfproperty name="lastName" type="string" default="" />
  <cfproperty name="gender" type="string" default="" />
  <cfproperty name="dateofbirth" type="string" default="" />
  <cfproperty name="hairColor" type="string" default="" />
  <!--- Pseudo-constructor --->
  <cfset variables.instance = {
    firstName = '', lastName = '', gender = '',
    dateofbirth = '', hairColor = ''
  } />
  <cffunction name="init" access="public" output="false"
    returntype="any" hint="I am the constructor method for the Person
    Class.">
    <cfargument name="firstName" required="true" type="String"
      default="" hint="I am the first name." />
    <cfargument name="lastName" required="true" type="String"
      default="" hint="I am the last name." />
    <cfargument name="gender" required="true" type="String"
      default="" hint="I am the gender." />
    <cfargument name="dateofbirth" required="true" type="String"
      default="" hint="I am the date of birth." />
    <cfargument name="hairColor" required="true" type="String"
      default="" hint="I am the hair color." />
    <!--- Set the initial values of the Bean --->
    <cfscript>
      setFirstName(arguments.firstName);
      setLastName(arguments.lastName);
      setGender(arguments.gender);
      setDateOfBirth(arguments.dateofbirth);
      setHairColor(arguments.hairColor);
    </cfscript>
```

```
    <cfreturn this />
</cffunction>


<!--- getters / accessors --->
<cffunction name="getFirstName" access="public"
  output="false" hint="I return the first name.">
  <cfreturn variables.instance.firstName />
</cffunction>


<cffunction name="getLastName" access="public"
  output="false" hint="I return the last name.">
  <cfreturn variables.instance.lastName />
</cffunction>


<cffunction name="getGender" access="public"
  output="false" hint="I return the gender.">
  <cfreturn variables.instance.gender />
</cffunction>


<cffunction name="getDateOfBirth" access="public"
  output="false" hint="I return the date of birth.">
  <cfreturn variables.instance.dateofbirth />
</cffunction>


<cffunction name="getHairColor" access="public"
  output="false" hint="I return the hair color.">
  <cfreturn variables.instance.hairColor />
</cffunction>


<!--- setters /mutators --->
<cffunction name="setFirstName" access="public"
  output="false" hint="I set the first name into the
  variables.instance scope.">
  <cfargument name="firstName" required="true"
    type="String" hint="I am the person's firstName." />
    <cfset variables.instance.firstName = arguments.firstName />
</cffunction>


<cffunction name="setLastName" access="public"
  output="false" hint="I set the last name into the
  variables.instance scope.">
  <cfargument name="lastName" required="true"
    type="String" hint="I am the person's lastName." />
    <cfset variables.instance.lastName = arguments.lastName />
</cffunction>
```

```
<cffunction name="setGender" access="public"
  output="false" hint="I set the gender into the
  variables.instance scope.">
  <cfargument name="gender" required="true"
    type="String" hint="I am the person's gender." />
    <cfset variables.instance.gender = arguments.gender />
</cffunction>

<cffunction name="setDateOfBirth" access="public"
  output="false" hint="I set the dateofbirth into the
  variables.instance scope.">
  <cfargument name="dateofbirth" required="true"
    type="String" hint="I am the person's dateofbirth." />
    <cfset variables.instance.dateofbirth =
      arguments.dateofbirth />
</cffunction>

<cffunction name="setHairColor" access="public"
  output="false" hint="I set the hairColor into the
  variables.instance scope.">
  <cfargument name="hairColor" required="true"
    type="String" hint="I am the person's hairColor." />
    <cfset variables.instance.hairColor = arguments.hairColor />
</cffunction>

<cffunction name="getFullName" access="public"
  output="false" hint="I return the full name of the person.">
  <cfset var strFullName = '' />
  <!---Concatenate the string values to return the full name.
    Here, we call the variables.instance values directly.
    You could also call the get methods, like so:
    getFirstName() & ' ' & getLastName()--->
    <cfset strFullName = variables.instance.firstName & ' ' &
      variables.instance.lastName />
  <cfreturn strFullName />
</cffunction>

<cffunction name="getAgeInYears" access="public"
  output="false" hint="I work out the age of the person in
  years based upon the current date.">
  <cfset var strAgeInYears = '' />
    <!---Calculate the difference in years using the person's
      stored date of birth and the current year.--->
    <cfset strAgeInYears = dateDiff('yyyy', getDateOfBirth(),
      now()) />
  <cfreturn strAgeInYears />
```

```
</cffunction>

<!--- utils --->
<cffunction name="getMemento" access="public"
  output="false" hint="I return a dumped struct of the
    variables.instance scope.">
  <cfreturn variables.instance />
</cffunction>
</cfcomponent>
```

Listing 3.15 – Adding useful 'helper' methods into `Person.cfc`

Thanks to the additional methods within the component, we are able to easily obtain the person's full name and current age without having to perform any calculations outside of the object itself.

Revising our UML diagram for the Person class, we can add in the two new methods, and ensure that the mutator/setter methods are set to private.

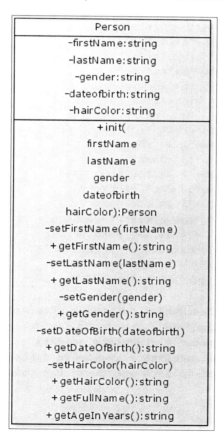

Implicit accessors

With the evolution of ColdFusion 9 we are able to write the same powerful, functional components, but with less code. In some instances, this may be due to the fact that we no longer need to write our core components in tag format, but also due to the powerful ability to have the accessor/getter and mutator/setter methods generated for you if required.

This is achieved from the `accessors` attribute within the main `component` tag. Following is a ColdFusion 9 specific version of our complete Person component:

```
<cfcomponent displayname="Person" output="false"
  hint="I am the Person Class." accessors="true">
  <cfproperty name="firstName" type="string"
    default="" setter="false" />
  <cfproperty name="lastName" type="string"
    default="" setter="false" />
  <cfproperty name="gender" type="string"
    default="" setter="false" />
  <cfproperty name="dateofbirth" type="string"
    default="" setter="false" />
  <cfproperty name="hairColor" type="string"
    default="" setter="false" />
  <cffunction name="init" access="public" output="false"
    returntype="any" hint="I am the constructor method for the
    Person Class.">
    <cfargument name="firstName" required="true" type="String"
      default="" hint="I am the first name." />
    <cfargument name="lastName" required="true" type="String"
      default="" hint="I am the last name." />
    <cfargument name="gender" required="true" type="String"
      default="" hint="I am the gender." />
    <cfargument name="dateofbirth" required="true" type="String"
      default="" hint="I am the date of birth." />
    <cfargument name="hairColor" required="true" type="String"
      default="" hint="I am the hair color." />
    <!--- Set the initial values of the Bean --->
    <cfscript>
      variables.firstName = arguments.firstName;
      variables.lastName = arguments.lastName;
      variables.gender = arguments.gender;
      variables.dateofbirth = arguments.dateofbirth;
      variables.hairColor = arguments.hairColor;
    </cfscript>
  <cfreturn this />
  </cffunction>
```

```
<!--- public methods --->
<cffunction name="getFullName" access="public" output="false"
  hint="I return the full name of the person.">
  <cfset var strFullName = '' />
<!---Concatenate the string values to return the full name.
  Here, we call the variables values directly.
  You could also call the get methods, like so:
  getFirstName() & ' ' & getLastName()--->
  <cfset strFullName = variables.firstName & ' ' &
    variables.lastName />
  <cfreturn strFullName />
</cffunction>

<cffunction name="getAgeInYears" access="public" output="false"
  hint="I work out the age of the person in years
  based upon the current date.">
  <cfset var strAgeInYears = '' />
    <cfset strAgeInYears = dateDiff('yyyy', getDateOfBirth(),
      now()) />
  <cfreturn strAgeInYears />
</cffunction>

<cffunction name="getMemento" access="public" output="false"
  hint="I return the variables scope.">
  <cfreturn variables />
</cffunction>
</cfcomponent>
```

Listing 3.16 – Using Implicit Accessors in `Person.cfc`

The first thing you may notice is the length of the component content in comparison to our previous version in Listing 3.15, which is now much shorter. You will also notice that there are no mutator/setter methods and no accessor/getter methods that deal with the property values directly. We do have our 'custom' methods as well as the `init()` constructor, but no other methods.

This is due to the `accessors` attribute, set at the top of the document. By including this attribute and setting the value to `true`, the getters and setters are generated for you.

By generating all methods this way, they are all set to public access, meaning that all setter methods would be available to access outside of the component; perfect for a read/write component, as we have already seen.

In our previous component in Listing 3.15, we created a read-only component, and opted to set all of our property values within the constructor method. This effectively removed the need for any setter methods at all, although we kept them in.

In Listing 3.16, both the getter and setter methods are generated automatically. To convert this component into a read-only object and remove the setter methods completely, we can restrict the setter methods from being created as per our example by setting the `setter="false"` attribute within each `cfproperty` tag. This tells ColdFusion not to generate any setters for these properties.

Following this, our `Person.cfc` UML diagram would now look as follows:

Person
–firstName:string
–lastName:string
–gender:string
–dateofbirth:string
–hairColor:string
+init(
firstName
lastName
gender
dateofbirth
hairColor):Person
+getFirstName():string
+getLastName():string
+getGender():string
+getDateOfBirth():string
+getHairColor():string
+getFullName():string
+getAgeInyears():string
+getMemento():any

When using the automatically-generated methods, the property values are stored and retrieved from the `variables` scope itself, whereas in our hand-written example, we were storing the values within `variables.instance`. To reflect this change, the code in Listing 3.16 was amended to reference only the `variables` scope, and not the `variables.instance` structure.

Listing 3.17 shows the same Person ColdFusion component using the implicit getters, written in pure script syntax.

```
component displayname="Person" hint="I am the Person Class."
  accessors="true"
{

  property name="firstName" type="string" default="" setter="false";
  property name="lastName" type="string" default="" setter="false";
  property name="gender" type="string" default="" setter="false";
  property name="dateofbirth" type="string" default=""
    setter="false";
  property name="hairColor" type="string" default="" setter="false";
  public any function init(
    required string firstName        = "", required string lastName =
"",
    required string gender = "", required string dateofbirth = "",
    required string hairColor = "")
    output = "false" hint="I am the constructor method for the
      Person Class."
  {
      /*
        Store the values into the variables scope.
        We do not have mutator/setter methods
        within this component, but we can set the
        values into the variables scope directly.
      */
      variables.firstName    = arguments.firstName;
      variables.lastName        = arguments.lastName;
      variables.gender       = arguments.gender;
      variables.dateofbirth  = arguments.dateofbirth;
      variables.hairColor       = arguments.hairColor;
    return (this);
  }
  public string function getFullName()
    output="false" hint="I return the full name of the person."
  {
    local.strFullName = variables.firstName & ' ' &
      variables.lastName;
    return local.strFullName;
  }
  public string function getAgeInYears()
    output="false" hint="I work out the age of the person in years
    based upon the current date."
  {
    local.strAgeInYears = dateDiff('yyyy', getDateOfBirth(), now());
    return local.strAgeInYears;
  }
  public any function getMemento()
```

```
        output="false" hint="I return the variables scope."
    {
      return variables;
    }
}
```

Listing 3.17 – `Person.cfc` written in script syntax (ColdFusion 9 only)

Summary

In this chapter, we have introduced the Bean into our ColdFusion object-oriented programming design pattern, and have understood that a Bean is a blueprint of an object, which we can create and populate at any time, and that this object represents a single record of data, or a specific entity.

By following the conventions in this chapter to create your ColdFusion Beans, using the get/set methods to access and populate your Bean's properties does require a little more typing to write the functions for each property.

However, this time will be well-spent when the application grows and becomes more complex. The benefits of writing your code with an object-oriented approach will soon become apparent, and they will strengthen when we introduce a framework to handle our code and objects for us, which we will cover later in this book.

Other topics we have covered in this chapter are:

- The benefit of using Beans
- Accessor/Getter methods
- Mutator/Setter methods
- Building and populating a Bean
- Implicit getters/setters in ColdFusion 9

4

Inheritance and
Object-Oriented Concepts

Now that we have built our components and looked at creating Bean objects, we can start to delve a little deeper and have a look at some of the core concepts involved in object-oriented programming.

The world of OOP can be laden with jargon, keywords, and concepts, some of which may be obvious. Others may be easily misunderstood or simply confusing.

In this chapter, we will take a look at a few of the key concepts that you may well experience within an object-oriented application, together with code examples to assist with understanding these ideas, starting with the concept of inheritance.

We will also look at the following:

- Polymorphism
- Composition
- Aggregation

What is Inheritance?

Inheritance is one of the primary concepts of object-oriented programming, and is when one object (a **child**) extends another object (the **parent**). By extending the parent object, the child object inherits the properties and methods of the parent object.

By using the concept of inheritance you can create a hierarchy of objects, beginning with general things and progressing to very specific objects. Let's use a real-world example, and envisage an e-commerce application.

Let's imagine that initially our online store sells only books, and as such we only have one single product object, Book.cfc. This component contains the relevant properties accessor and mutator methods to read and write our information relating to our book products.

The UML diagram of the object could look something like this:

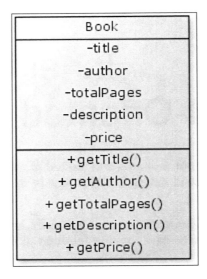

At the moment, this Book object is perfectly suited for our application. It contains exactly the right properties we need to provide information about our books. It would also be incredibly easy to amend the object if we needed to add any additional properties for the product, for example, a barcode or ISBN number.

Now, imagine that our business has really taken off and we've decided to enhance our shopping site and sell different products; we now want to branch out and sell not only books, but also DVDs.

It's fantastic news that our business is doing so well, and that we are expanding to offer more products to our customers. However, this does have an immediate impact on our underlying application and, more importantly, the product objects.

Once again, let's view a UML diagram of our new DVD object to help visualize the issue:

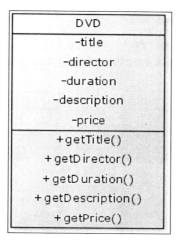

As you can see more or less straight away, there are major similarities between the two products and properties that are common to both, namely the title, description, and price for each product.

Of course, there is nothing to stop us from simply creating this new object as pictured in the UML diagram, and having the Book and DVD objects containing similar methods and properties within our application. We are still able to set and read the properties for our products, and pass them throughout our application as bean objects.

Avoiding code duplication

However, let's now imagine that we have broadened our product levels once more and we now sell CDs, Calendars, electronic gadgets, and so on from our web application.

We have already seen duplicated code when we introduced our second product object. The following diagram is an example of our revised product range:

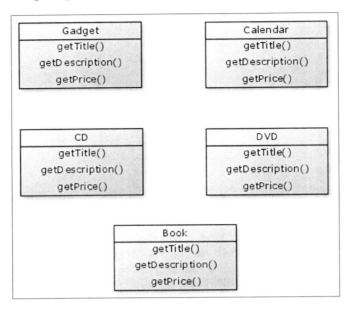

Excluding any extra methods and properties that the individual products may have in the previous product visualization, we can now clearly see the similarities between the products; they all share title, description, and price properties and methods. To this extent, we can now see the highlighted levels of code duplication within our application.

To avoid this code duplication and to help streamline the structure of our application where possible, we can start to utilize the concept of inheritance.

We can create a brand new **Base** class (or **super-component**), into which any common/shared code can be placed. Any properties or methods within this new component would then be made available to the more specific classes (also known as **subclasses**) as they inherit the super-component.

Inheriting our products

We have seen from our earlier UML diagrams that our products all contain similar methods. We will ultimately place these methods within our new Base product class, and keep the more specific product methods within their individual objects.

Let's start by looking at another simple UML diagram to help understand and visualize this inheritance.

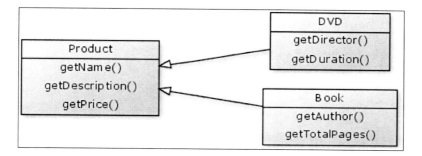

You can see the clear separation of methods (and inherently their properties) from our products that will be placed into our Product Base class. The remaining methods that relate to the specific products stay within that product's specific object.

The concept of inheritance is also clearly visualized in the previous diagram in the form of the clear arrowheads connecting the objects. We can now say that the DVD object will inherit the Product object, and the Book object will also inherit the Product Base class.

Create a new file called `Product.cfc` and place it within the following location: `com/packtApp/oop/beans`. Add the code from Listing 4.1 into the component to create our Base class.

```
<cfcomponent displayname="Product"
        output="false"
        hint="I am the Product Base Class.">

  <cfset variables.instance = structNew() />

  <cffunction name="init" access="public"
        output="false" returntype="any"
        hint="I am the constructor method for
            the Product Base class.">

    <cfargument name="name" required="true"
            type="String" default=""
```

```
            hint="I am the name of the product." />

    <cfargument name="description" required="true"
          type="String" default=""
          hint="I am a description for the product." />

    <cfargument name="price" required="true"
          type="String" default=""
          hint="I am the price." />

      <cfscript>
        variables.instance.name
          = arguments.name;

        variables.instance.description
          = arguments.description;

        variables.instance.price
          = arguments.price;
      </cfscript>
    <cfreturn this />
  </cffunction>

  <!--- getters / accessors --->
  <cffunction name="getName" access="public"
        output="false"
        hint="I return the name of the product.">
    <cfreturn variables.instance.name />
  </cffunction>

  <cffunction name="getDescription" access="public"
        output="false"
        hint="I return a decsription of the product.">
    <cfreturn variables.instance.description />
  </cffunction>

  <cffunction name="getPrice" access="public"
        output="false"
        hint="I return the price of the product.">
    <cfreturn variables.instance.price />
  </cffunction>

</cfcomponent>
```

Listing 4.1 - Creating our Product Base class

The code in Listing 4.1 contains the complete code for the Product Base class, which contains four public methods: the `init()` constructor method, and the three getter/accessor methods to return the values of the object's properties: name, description, and price respectively.

This particular example is a read-only bean as we haven't specified any publicly accessible setter/mutator methods, although you can add these if you wish, as we had included these in the previous chapter.

Now that we have our Base class (or super-component), we need to redefine our Book object to inherit the methods and properties from our `Product.cfc`.

ColdFusion provides an incredibly simple way to specify object inheritance within your components, which is through the use of the `extends` attribute within the `cfcomponent` tag.

The following code in Listing 4.2 shows the core of `Book.cfc`, which now inherits the Product Base class.

```
<cfcomponent displayname="Book"
    output="false"
    hint="I am the Book Class."
    extends="Product">

  <cfproperty name="author"      type="string" default="" />
  <cfproperty name="totalPages" type="string" default="" />
  <cfproperty name="name"        type="string" default="" />
  <cfproperty name="description" type="string" default="" />
  <cfproperty name="price"       type="string" default="" />

  <cfset variables.instance = structNew() />


</cfcomponent>
```

Listing 4.2 – Inheriting our Base class in our Book object

With thanks to the single `extends=""` attribute, `Book.cfc` will now have the ability to inherit from our Product super-component.

Let's now add our `init()` constructor method into the Book component.

The code in Listing 4.3 shows our constructor method, which we'll call when instantiating our Book object.

As we have seen in previous chapters, we are passing the parameters into the init() method, which we will use to set the values of the properties.

You can see that we are directly setting the values for the author and totalPages properties into the variables.instance structure within the Book component.

```
<cffunction name="init" access="public"
    output="false" returntype="any"
    hint="I am the constructor method
        for the Book Class.">

  <cfargument name="author" required="true"
        type="String" default=""
        hint="I am the author of the book." />

  <cfargument name="totalPages" required="true"
        type="String" default=""
        hint="I am the total number of
            pages within the book." />

  <cfargument name="name" required="true"
        type="String" default=""
        hint="I am the name of the book." />

  <cfargument name="description"    required="true"
        type="String" default=""
        hint="I am a description for the book." />

  <cfargument name="price" required="true"
        type="String" default=""
        hint="I am the price." />

    <cfscript>
      // Set the values of the Book-specific properties
      variables.instance.author
        = arguments.author;

      variables.instance.totalPages
        = arguments.totalPages;

      /*
      Run the constructor method within the Base Product class
      Here, we use the super prefix to
      override the Book init() method and
      to use the constructor within the Base class.
```

```
    */
    super.init(
        name        = arguments.name,
        description = arguments.description,
        price       = arguments.price
        );
    </cfscript>

  <cfreturn this />

</cffunction>

<!--- getters / accessors --->
<cffunction name="getAuthor" access="public"
        output="false"
        hint="I am the author.">
  <cfreturn variables.instance.author />
</cffunction>

<cffunction name="getTotalPages" access="public"
        output="false"
        hint="I am the total number of
                pages within the book.">
  <cfreturn variables.instance.totalPages />
</cffunction>
```

Listing 4.3 – Including the init() constructor

The Super keyword

What is important to note in the prior code listing is the process by which we set the values for the properties within the Base class.

Overriding methods

When using the concept of inheritance within our object-oriented application, the child objects (or subtypes) inherit all of the methods and properties contained within the parent (super component or Base class), as we have previously mentioned.

If a child object already contains a method with the same name as one written within the Base class, the method within the child object is used, overriding that from the parent object.

In our current code, both the Book child component and the Product parent component contain an `init()` constructor method, both of them used to set the values of the properties within each object.

However, although the Book object inherits the methods from the Product class, if we were to call `objBook.init()` to instantiate our object, only the constructor method from the Book component would be run.

We still need to run the `init()` method within the Product parent class and we are still able to call the overridden method by using the **super** prefix, as seen in Listing 4.3, which now allows access to the method contained within the parent object.

As the constructor method within the Product Base class requires the three arguments, we are able to then pass them through using the super keyword.

Instantiating our products

We can create as many child objects as required to fulfill our many different products in similar fashion to the code examples for the Book object.

In the following code examples, we have the Book and DVD components, both of which extend the Product Base class.

To populate the objects, we simply need to instantiate the components and send through the parameters, as seen in Listing 4.4.

```
<cfset objBook =
  createObject('component',
  'com.packtApp.oop.beans.Book')
  .init(
    author      = 'John Farrar',
    totalPages  = '382',
    name        = 'ColdFusion 9 Developer Tutorial',
    description = 'Create robust professional web
             applications with ColdFusion',
    price       = '30.99'
  ) />

<cfdump var="#objBook#" />

<cfset objDVD =
  createObject('component',
  'com.packtApp.oop.beans.DVD')
  .init(
    director    = 'Steven Iceberg',
```

```
duration     = '220 minutes',
name         = 'Raising Wisconsin',
description  = 'One man against the world.',
price        = '14.75'
) />

<cfdump var="#objDVD#" />
```

Listing 4.4 – Instantiating our product objects

The resulting output from the code in Listing 4.4 clearly shows the population of the properties within not only the child component, but also the parent component, as you can see in the following image:

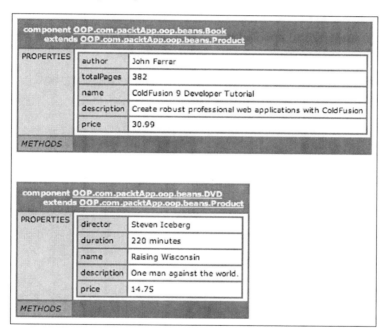

The three shared properties contained within the Product Base class are populated, as are the values of the properties relating to the individual product object.

The inheritance hierarchy

The concept of inheritance displays an effective method of sharing related code across numerous components.

Although we are free to use the option of the `extends` attribute when writing our ColdFusion components to inherit and use methods from other components (in fact, we use the process in *Chapter 7* to share a single common method amongst multiple components), in the world of object-oriented programming we need to follow a few specific guidelines to ensure we are implementing inheritance and not merely sharing code.

Specialization

An easy way to understand specialization is to visualize the children and parent objects as a ladder, where each rung is a level of objects.

In our e-commerce application, we could use the following diagram:

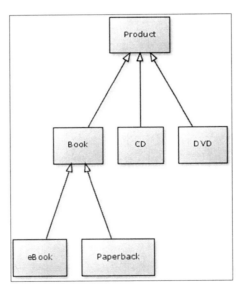

In the previous image, we have three tiers of objects. At the top is the parent object or super-component. If were to move from the top tier travelling down our object hierarchy, each level we reach contains an object that is a more specialized version of the one before it.

For example, Book, CD, and DVD are more specialized versions of the Product object.

We can add x amount of levels to our hierarchy, and continue to create more specialized objects, as seen here. E-book and Paperback are more specialized versions of our Book object. With every layer we navigate downwards, we create a more specific object.

Likewise, this works in reverse, moving from the bottom of the structure to the top. As we travel up our object ladder, every component we see is a more generalized version of its predecessor. Book is a more generalized version of e-book and Paperback. Product is a more generalized version of our Book, CD, and DVD objects.

And so, true inheritance in OOP terms must imply specialization.

The "IS A" relationship

Another method to test for true inheritance in terms of object-oriented programming is to be able to define a correct "IS A" relationship between the components. Looking at our application structure, for example, we can say that:

- Book IS A Product
- CD IS A Product, as is DVD
- eBook IS A Book
- Paperback IS A Book

Although you may be using the `extends` attribute to inherit methods and properties from other components, if you can confirm that your object structure and hierarchy match these two criteria, you can happily say you have incorporated true inheritance into your applications.

Polymorphism

Polymorphism is another important concept in the world of object-oriented programming, and is relatively simple to understand.

Polymorphism occurs as a side effect of inheritance. Essentially, it means that you can treat a child object and its inherited methods and properties in exactly the same way you would treat the parent object's methods and properties.

Consider the following code example, in which we output the name property of each product using the objects we have instantiated in Listing 4.4.

```
<cfoutput>
  Book Name: #objBook.getName()#<br />
  DVD Name: #objDVD.getName()#
</cfoutput>
```

Listing 4.5 – Displaying each product name

All of our child objects inherited the `getName()` method from within our parent object, the Product Base class. In the previous code example, each child object calls the same inherited method, but returns a different result for each call.

Essentially, this means that the inherited method is polymorphic, as it behaves in exactly the same manner for every object as it does for its parent.

Composition

The next basic concept of object-oriented programming to introduce is that of composition.

Composition is the concept that an object cannot exist without its composite parts. In essence, it is the process of creating an object from a combination of other objects.

A common way to show this example is in the form of a car. Many objects go into making a car. Some of them are 'optional extras' and trimmings from the dealership such as a cup holder or satellite navigation system, whereas others are crucial for the existence of the car, such as an engine or wheels.

The following UML diagram provides another helpful visualization of composition:

Composition is represented in UML as a filled diamond shape and a solid black line.

An engine on its own is just an engine. In true object-oriented practices, as an object it cannot exist without the car such as its parent object. Similarly, a car is an object, but is nothing without an engine.

On their own, these objects are not of much use. Combining them together, the individual components compose an object that is incredibly useful and useable.

The "HAS A" Relationship

One method of confirming you have true composition is again checking the relationship between the components.

Simply referred to as a "HAS A" relationship, in this example a car "HAS A" engine. An engine does not have a car.

The following code contains the entire Car object component. Create a new file called Car.cfc and save it to the following directory: com/packtApp/oop/beans. Insert the code from Listing 4.6 into Car.cfc.

```
<cfcomponent displayname="Car"
        output="false"
        hint="I am the Car Class.">

    <cfproperty name="engine" type="any" default="" />

    <cfset variables.instance = structNew() />

    <cffunction name="init" access="public"
            output="false" returntype="any"
            hint="I am the constructor method
                for the Car Class.">

        <cfset variables.instance.engine =
            createObject('component', 'engine') />

        <cfreturn this />

    </cffunction>

    <!--- getters / accessors --->
    <cffunction name="getEngine" access="public"
            output="false" hint="I return the engine.">

        <cfreturn variables.instance.engine />

    </cffunction>

</cfcomponent>
```

Listing 4.6 – A Car object, which requires an engine

You can see from the code in Listing 4.6 that the Car object instantiates and sets the Engine object itself within the init() constructor method. This highlights the fact that the Car cannot exist without its composite objects, in this simple example the Engine.

Create a new file called `Engine.cfc` and save it within the following location: `com/packtApp/oop/beans`. Copy the code from Listing 4.7 into `Engine.cfc` to create the composite component required by our Car object.

```
<cfcomponent displayname="Engine"
        output="false"
        hint="I am the Engine Class.">

    <cfset variables.instance = structNew() />

    <cffunction name="init" access="public"
            output="false" returntype="any"
            hint="I am the constructor method
                for the Engine Class.">

        <cfreturn this />

    </cffunction>

</cfcomponent>
```

Listing 4.7 – An Engine object, required for the car to exist

In this example, the Engine object itself is incredibly simple. Most likely within a real-world application, any composite objects would include more methods and functions than purely a constructor method.

Let's instantiate our Car object to see the composition in action.

The following code in Listing 4.8 contains the `createObject()` method to instantiate the Car object, followed by a `cfdump` to view the object itself.

```
<cfset objCar =
    createObject('component',
    'com.packtApp.oop.beans.Car')
    .init() />

<cfdump var="#objCar#" />
```

Listing 4.8 – Instantiating the Car object

Our Car object requires no arguments or parameters, and so we do not need to send any values into the constructor method. We understand that the Car object will create its required Engine object and set the Engine into its `variables.instance` structure.

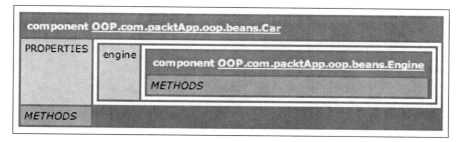

The output from the `cfdump` tag in Listing 4.8 can be seen in the previous image, in which you can clearly see the Engine object nested within the properties of our Car object, created as a requirement for our Car to exist.

Implied ownership

The concept of composition implies a certain level of ownership. When our Car object is destroyed, so are the contained objects and its composite parts. No more engine, no more wheels, no more pine-scented air freshener.

Aggregation

In comparison to composition in which an object can only exist if all of its composite parts also exist, the concept of aggregation is not as strict. Instead, an aggregated object can reference other objects, but it *does not need* them to exist.

We can see a simple example of aggregation in action if we again reference our Car object. Unlike composition, where our car needed an engine to exist (after all, what is a car without an engine), a car can have a driver, but it *does not need* the driver to exist.

Let's revise our current `Car.cfc` component to handle the possibility of managing a Driver object.

```
<cfcomponent displayname="Car"
        output="false"
        hint="I am the Car Class.">

  <cfproperty name="engine" type="any" default="" />
  <cfproperty name="driver" type="any" default="" />

  <cfset variables.instance = structNew() />

  <cffunction name="init" access="public"
```

```
        output="false" returntype="any"
        hint="I am the constructor method
            for the Car Class.">

    <cfargument name="driver" required="false"
            type="Any"
            hint="I am a driver object." />

        <cfset variables.instance.engine
            = createObject('component', 'engine') />

        <cfif structKeyExists(arguments, 'driver')>
            <cfset variables.instance.driver
                = arguments.driver />
        </cfif>

    <cfreturn this />

</cffunction>

<!--- getters / accessors --->
<cffunction name="getEngine" access="public"
        output="false"
        hint="I return the engine.">

    <cfreturn variables.instance.engine />

</cffunction>

<cffunction name="getDriver" access="public"
        output="false"
        hint="I return the driver.">

    <cfreturn variables.instance.driver />

</cffunction>

<!--- public methods --->
<cffunction name="hasDriver" access="public"
        returntype="boolean" output="false"
        hint="I check to see if a driver exists.">

    <cfreturn structKeyExists(variables.instance, 'driver') />

</cffunction>

</cfcomponent>
```

Listing 4.9 – Revising our Car object to accept a driver

As you can see highlighted in Listing 4.9, `Car.cfc` has received a few amendments to handle the possible addition of a Driver object.

We have added in a non-required argument to the constructor method into which we can send the Driver object if we wish to. If it does exist within the `arguments` scope, then we can set the object into the `variables.instance` structure.

If a Driver object has not been passed into the constructor method, our Car object will still be built, complete with its required engine object.

We have also added in a public method to check for the existence of the Driver object, which will return a Boolean true/false value.

Let's now create our simple Driver object. Create a new file called `Driver.cfc` within `com/packtApp/oop/beans` and add the following code from Listing 4.10 into the component.

```
<cfcomponent displayname="Driver"
      output="false"
      hint="I am the Driver Class.">

  <cfproperty name="name" type="string" default="" />
  <cfproperty name="age"  type="string" default="" />

  <cfset variables.instance = structNew() />

  <cffunction name="init" access="public"
        output="false" returntype="any"
        hint="I am the constructor method
           for the Driver Class.">

    <cfargument name="name" required="true"
          type="String"
          hint="I am the name of the driver." />

    <cfargument name="age" required="true"
          type="String"
          hint="I am the age of the driver." />

    <cfscript>
      variables.instance.name = arguments.name;
      variables.instance.age  = arguments.age;
    </cfscript>
```

```
      <cfreturn this />

   </cffunction>


   <!--- getters / accessors --->
   <cffunction name="getName" access="public"
         output="false"
         hint="I return the name of the driver.">

      <cfreturn variables.instance.name />

   </cffunction>


   <cffunction name="getAge" access="public"
         output="false"
         hint="I return the age of the driver.">

      <cfreturn variables.instance.age />

   </cffunction>

</cfcomponent>
```

Listing 4.10 – A Driver object

In our example, the Driver object is incredibly simple and requires only two properties; the name and age of the driver, with a getter/accessor method to obtain the value of each property.

Let's create two instances of the Car object, one of which will receive a Driver. The code in Listing 4.11 contains the relevant code to instantiate the objects.

```
<!--- Instantiate the Driver object --->
<cfset objDriver=
   createObject('component',
   'com.packtApp.oop.beans.Driver')
   .init(
     name    = 'Stevey Jay',
     age     = '31'
   ) />


<!---    Pass the Driver object into our Car object.--->
<cfset objCar =
   createObject('component',
   'com.packtApp.oop.beans.Car')
```

```
  .init(
    driver = objDriver
  ) />

<cfdump var="#objCar#" />

<cfoutput>

<cfif objCar.hasDriver()>
This car is being driven by #objDriver.getName()#,
who is #objDriver.getAge()# years old.
<cfelse>
The car is not being driven at the moment.
</cfif>

</cfoutput>
```

Listing 4.11 – Instantiating our Car objects with an optional Driver object

In Listing 4.11, we are first creating our Driver object, before creating our Car object, into which we send the Driver as a parameter.

Running a `cfdump` we are able to obtain a visual of the Car object and its properties, which we can see in the following image.

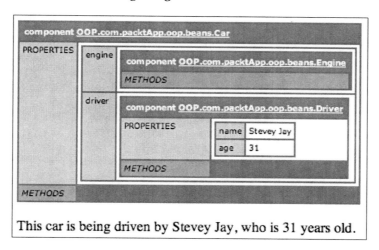

We then make a request to the `hasDriver()` method within our Car object to check for the existence of the Driver object, after which we are displaying either the driver information or a generic message to inform that the Car has no driver.

We can amend the code by not sending the Driver object into the Car constructor method (as follows).

```
<cfset objCar =
  createObject('component',
  'com.packtApp.oop.beans.Car')
  .init( ) />

<cfdump var="#objCar#" />

<cfoutput>

<cfif objCar.hasDriver()>
This car is being driven by #objDriver.getName()#,
who is #objDriver.getAge()# years old.
<cfelse>
The car is not being driven at the moment.
</cfif>

</cfoutput>
```

Listing 4.12 –Revising the code to not send through a Driver

Running the previous revised code from Listing 4.12, we obtain the following output:

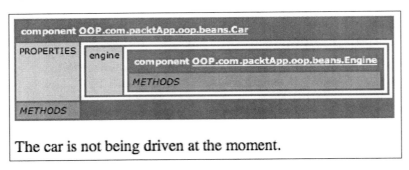

Unlike composition, the Car object can still be created without the Driver object, as it does not require it to be instantiated. We have added in methods to check for its existence and to return it if required, but the object will still function properly without it.

Summary

In this chapter, we have explored the concept of inheritance within an object-oriented application. We have looked at the possibility of sharing common code amongst your components to reduce code duplication, but we have also investigated a little further to better understand the requirements for true inheritance in the world of OOP.

We have also looked into:

- The hierarchy of components and objects during inheritance
- Polymorphism as a side-effect of inheritance
- The difference between composition and aggregation

5
Data Access Objects

Our application structure is starting to take shape, and the addition of Beans and the benefit of using these blueprints has already started to become apparent.

In this chapter, we will follow on our journey into ColdFusion OOP design patterns, and investigate the use of Data Access Objects with our application.

We will also look into the following:

- Understanding what a Data Access Object is
- Creating database interactions
- Storing objects in memory

What is a Data Access Object?

A **Data Access Object**, also known as a **DAO**, is a form of an object-oriented design pattern that allows you to separate data access from standard business logic within your application. Primarily, the DAO gives you the ability to perform updates and interactions with your database from a single file, your DAO file itself.

As we have seen in *Chapter 3*, the Bean objects hold values for a single record of data. The Data Access Objects work in harmony with the Bean objects and update a single record or row within a larger data store—this could be an XML file, text file, or any other form of storage, but more commonly a database.

 Traditionally, Data Access Objects only ever deal with a single record at a time.

Traditionally, a DAO will contain four methods that allow you to do the following:

- Create/insert a record
- Read/select a record
- Update a record
- Delete a record

The 'big four' methods within a DAO are commonly referred to as **CRUD** methods (**C**reate, **R**ead, **U**pdate, and **D**elete) and perform the basic SQL database functions; Insert, Select, Update, and Delete.

Creating a Data Access Object

For our introduction into Data Access Objects, we'll create a small application to query, read, and update a database table containing information on users; this could be applied to a real-world example such as a login form, or a user management console.

We will be accessing the data from a table within our database, called `tbl_Users`, which contains relatively basic information for each entry. Here, you can see a UML diagram of the `User.cfc` bean, which has been created to reflect the columns and interact with the values from the table.

User
-ID
-firstName
-lastName
-username
-password
-emailAddress
+init():User
+getID():Number
+getFirstName():String
+getLastName():String
+getUsername():String
+getPassword():String
+getFullName():String

You can see from the UML diagram that we have a getter/accessor method for each property within the bean, and we also have a simple helper function, getFullName(), which will concatenate the user's first and last names into a single string. We also have a public setter/mutator function for each property, although these haven't been included in this diagram for simplicity.

The User bean will play an incredibly important role used in conjunction with our User Data Access Object. As the blueprint for each user, the User bean will be populated with information returned from the database queries within the DAO.

If we consider the CRUD statements that we would like to include into our User DAO, we could expect the UML diagram of our object to look similar to this:

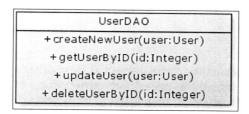

The four main methods written within the UML diagram would satisfy our basic requirements for our CRUD methods, which are:

- createNewUser()
- getUserByID()
- updateUser()
- deleteUser()

Let's start by building the core foundation for the UserDAO.cfc. As with all of our ColdFusion components, we need to define the init() constructor method to instantiate the object for use in our application.

Create a new file called UserDAO.cfc in the following directory from your webroot: 'com.packtApp.oop.dataAccess.UserDAO.cfc', and copy the following code into the file:

```
<cfcomponent displayname="UserDAO" output="false" hint="I am the
  UserDAO Class.">
  <!--- Pseudo-constructor --->
  <cfset variables.instance = {
    datasource  = ''
  } />
```

```
<cffunction name="init" access="public" output="false"
  returntype="any" hint="I am the constructor method or the
  UserDAO Class.">
  <cfargument name="datasource" required="true"
    type="com.packtApp.oop.beans.Datasource" hint="I am the
    datasource object." />
    <!--- Set the initial values of the Bean --->
    <cfscript>
      variables.instance.datasource = arguments.datasource;
    </cfscript>
  <cfreturn this />
</cffunction>
<!--- PUBLIC METHODS --->
</cfcomponent>
```

Listing 5.1 – `UserDAO.cfc`

Initially, the layout and structure of this object is incredibly similar to any other CFC we have built so far. We set up the pseudo-constructor, and we have the `init()` constructor method to set any variables upon instantiation.

As with other constructor methods, we are sending through a value to set and use throughout our DAO.

Our Data Access Object's purpose is to interact with a given datasource. As such, we need to let the DAO know the details for the datasource we wish to connect to, as specified within the ColdFusion administrator.

We could simply pass through a string variable that contains the name of the datasource, and save that value within the `variables.instance` scope. However, database connectivity may be restricted to user access and so may require a username and password to connect from within our code.

These could also be sent through as separate string values, but we could easily incorporate these into their own object, which acts as a blueprint for any datasource connections. It is this object that we are sending through into the DAO `init()` method.

You can see from the `cfargument` tag in Listing 5.1, that we can force the `type` attribute to expect a specific object by setting it to the location of the object within our application file structure.

The structure for our Datasource bean itself is incredibly simple, and contains three simple methods to access the name of the datasource, a username, and a password.

The UML diagram for the Class is represented as follows:

```
<cfcomponent displayname="Datasource" output="false"
  hint="I am the Datasource Class.">
  <cfproperty name="DSName" type="string" default="" />
  <cfproperty name="username" type="string" default="" />
  <cfproperty name="password" type="string" default="" />
  <!--- Pseudo-constructor --->
  <cfset variables.instance = {
    DSName     = '', username  = '', password  = ''
  } />
  <cffunction name="init" access="public" output="false"
    returntype="any" hint="I am the constructor method for the
    Datasource Class.">
    <cfargument name="DSName" required="true" type="String"
      hint="I am the name of the datasource." />
    <cfargument name="username" required="true" type="String"
      default="" hint="I am the username required to access
      the datasource." />
    <cfargument name="password" required="true" type="String"
      default="" hint="I am the password required to access
      the datasource." />
      <!--- Set the initial values of the Bean --->
      <cfscript>
        variables.instance.DSName   = arguments.DSName;
        variables.instance.username = arguments.username;
        variables.instance.password = arguments.password;
      </cfscript>
    <cfreturn this />
```

```
    </cffunction>
    <!--- getters / accessors --->
    <cffunction name="getDSName" access="public" output="false"
      hint="I return the name of the datasource.">
      <cfreturn variables.instance.DSName />
    </cffunction>
    <cffunction name="getUsername" access="public" output="false"
      hint="I return the username required to access the datasource.">
      <cfreturn variables.instance.username />
    </cffunction>
    <cffunction name="getPassword" access="public" output="false"
      hint="I return the password required to access the datasource.">
      <cfreturn variables.instance.password />
    </cffunction>
  </cfcomponent>
```

Listing 5.2 – `Datasource.cfc`

Now that we have a Datasource bean, we have the blueprint for any datasource, and so can reuse this object throughout our entire application and instantiate a new object for each datasource that we may have running behind our code.

Here, we first instantiate the Datasource object using the connection details to the datasource from the ColdFusion administrator, and then send that datasource object into the `UserDAO` object `init()` method.

```
    <!--- Instantiate the Datasource object. --->
    <cfset objDatasource = createObject('component',
      'com.packtApp.oop.beans.Datasource').init(
      DSName='CFOOP', username='<username>', password='<password>') />
    <!---Instantiate the UserDAO object, and pass in the Datasource
      object.--->
    <cfset objUserDAO = createObject('component',
      com.packtApp.oop.dataAccess.UserDAO').init(
      datasource=objDataSource) />
```

Listing 5.3 – Instantiating the `UserDAO` object

The technique of sending one object into another like this is known as **dependency injection**, which we will cover in a little more detail later within this chapter.

The create method

Now that we have the basis for our Data Access Object created, let's start adding the methods that will satisfy our basic CRUD operations.

The first to implement will be our method to create a new record.

The `createNewuser()` method within the DAO is essentially nothing more than a `cfquery` tag running an INSERT statement into the `tbl_Users` table.

Let's add the following code into the `userDAO.cfc` file underneath the constructor method:

```
<!--- CREATE --->
<cffunction name="createNewUser" access="public" output="false"
  returntype="Numeric" hint="I insert a new record into the
  database.">
  <cfargument name="user" required="true"
    type="com.packtApp.oop.beans.User" hint="I am the User bean." />
  <cfset var qInsert     = '' />
  <cfset var insertResult = 0 />
    <cfquery name="qInsert"
      datasource="#variables.instance.datasource.getDSName()#"
      username="#variables.instance.datasource.getUsername()#"
      password="#variables.instance.datasource.getPassword()#"
      result="insertResult">
      INSERT INTO tbl_Users(
          firstName, lastName, username, password, emailAddress)
      VALUES(
        <cfqueryparam cfsqltype="cf_sql_varchar"
        value="#arguments.user.getFirstName()#" />,
        <cfqueryparam cfsqltype="cf_sql_varchar"
        value="#arguments.user.getLastName()#" />,
        <cfqueryparam cfsqltype="cf_sql_varchar"
        value="#arguments.user.getUsername()#" />,
        <cfqueryparam cfsqltype="cf_sql_varchar"
        value="#arguments.user.getPassword()#" />,
        <cfqueryparam cfsqltype="cf_sql_varchar"
        value="#arguments.user.getEmailAddress()#" />
      )
    </cfquery>
  <!---Here, we return the generatedKey value, which is an
    auto-generated value from mySQL.--->
  <cfreturn insertResult.generatedKey />
</cffunction>
```

Listing 5.4 – The `createNewUser()` method

The INSERT statement itself is fairly standard SQL, calling the column names within the database we wish to insert data into.

The most important thing to note here is from where we obtain the values to insert into the table. For our one and only argument in this method, we are passing in the User object, which contains the data we wish to insert into the database to create our new record.

Using the getter/accessor methods within the User bean, we are able to obtain each value to use in the SQL statement, which are wrapped within a `cfqueryparam` tag. The `cfsqltype` attribute for each value is set to match the datatype of the value within the database, to aid with security and datatype validation.

Our `createNewUser()` method is returning the value of the generated primary key for the new record. In this example, this is possible using the `generatedKey` reference, which is the value generated from the MySQL database.

We can use that reference to create a populated User bean, having obtained the information from the database using the next of our core CRUD methods, a read method.

Storing a new user

Let's look at a practical example of creating a new user using the Data Access Object. We'll create a basic HTML form that submits the user data we want to capture. Once the form is submitted, we'll save the data into the database and generate a User bean populated with the information.

Create a new file and save it as `addNewUser.cfm`. Add the following code into the template:

```
<!---Check to see if the form has been submitted.--->
<cfif structKeyExists(FORM, 'submitUser_btn')>
</cfif>
<form name="createUser" action="addNewUser.cfm" method="POST">
  <label for="firstName">First name:</label>
  <input type="text" name="firstName" /><br />
  <label for="lastName">Surname:</label>
  <input type="text" name="lastName" /><br />
  <label for="lastName">Username:</label>
  <input type="text" name="username" /><br />
  <label for="password">Password:</label>
  <input type="password" name="password" /><br />
  <label for="emailAddress">Email:</label>
  <input type="text" name="emailAddress" /><br />
  <input type="submit" name="submitUser_btn" value="Create User" />
</form>
```

Listing 5.5 – `addNewUser.cfm`

In the previous code listing, we have a simple form to capture our user information. In this instance, the names of the form input elements also match the names of the properties within the User bean and the database table; this will make it easier to handle the data.

Between the `cfif` tags, add the following code to handle our database transaction and the creation of the User bean:

```
<cfif structKeyExists(FORM, 'submitUser_btn')>
    <!--- Instantiate the Datasource object. --->
    <cfset objDatasource =           createObject('component',
        'com.packtApp.oop.beans.Datasource').init(
        DSName='CFOOP', username='<your dsn username>',
        password='<your dsn password>') />

    <!---Instantiate the UserDAO object, and pass in the Datasource
        object.--->
    <cfset objUserDAO = createObject('component',
        'com.packtApp.oop.dataAccess.UserDAO').init(
        datasource=objDataSource) />

    <!---Populate a new User bean with the data submitted
        in the form.--->
    <cfset objUserBean = createObject('component',
        'com.packtApp.oop.beans.User').init(
        argumentCollection=FORM) />

    <!---Dump the User Bean so we can see it populated with
        the FORM data.--->
    <cfdump var="#objUserBean#" label="New User Bean" />

    <!---Send the new User bean into the UserDAO to create a new
        database entry, returning the generated key of the
        new record.--->
    <cfset intNewID = objUserDAO.createNewUser(user=objUserBean) />
    <!--- Set the new ID into the User Bean --->
    <cfset objUserBean.setID(intNewID) />

    <!---Dump the User Bean so we can see it completely
        populated now.--->
    <cfdump var="#objUserBean#" label="Revised New User Bean" />
</cfif>
```

Listing 5.6 – Form handler functionality in `addNewUser.cfm`

So, what are we doing once the form has been submitted?

Firstly, we are creating the instances of the Datasource object and the `UserDAO` object.

As these are both **singleton** objects, these would be very well suited to be instantiated and stored within the `Application` scope within your `onApplicationStart()` method, which would ensure their availability throughout the entire application and thereby reducing the overhead required to create these objects on every page they may be needed.

A singleton object is essentially an object that only requires a single instance within your application. Created only once during application start up, it does not need to be amended or revised, and typically exists for the entire duration of an application.

After the instantiation of the two singleton objects, we create an instance of the User bean. As the form element names matched the names of the bean properties, we do not need to match every one individually, and so here we are able to send the entire form into the `init()` method as an argument collection.

We do not yet have the ID for the User, and so a dump of the User bean shows that the ID property is still using the default value of '0'.

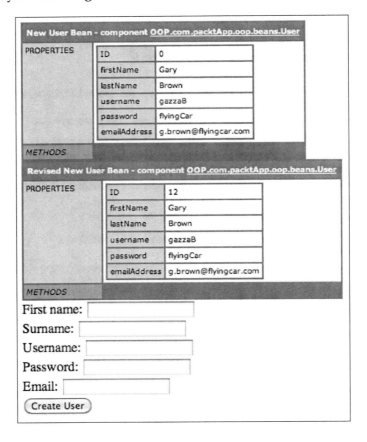

Next, we pass the freshly-created User bean into the `createNewUser()` method, which, as we have seen, will gather each property value and insert these into the database returning the generated ID of the new database record, which we will assign to the variable `intNewID`.

Now that we have the ID for the record, we can use the setter method to set the ID into the User bean object, and dumping the bean once more we can see the complete populated bean object, which now contains the ID of the record within the database.

The read method

Now that we are able to insert a single row of data into the database, we need the ability to retrieve it again.

Remembering that typically the CRUD methods deal with a single record at any time, the most logical way to obtain a record is to use its ID or primary key value. Essentially, a read method allows us to run a SELECT statement on the database, and pull out a single row of data based upon the WHERE clause, which in this case is the ID of the specific record we want to obtain.

Let's add the code for our `getUserByID()` method into the `userDAO.cfc`:

```
<!--- READ --->
<cffunction name="getUserByID" access="public" output="false"
  hint="I return a Person bean populated with details of a
  specific user.">
  <cfargument name="userID" required="true" type="Numeric"
    hint="I am the ID of the user you wish to search for." />
  <cfset var qSearch     = '' />
  <cfset var objPerson   = '' />
    <cfquery name="qSearch"
      datasource="#variables.instance.datasource.getDSName()#"
      username="#variables.instance.datasource.getUsername()#"
      password="#variables.instance.datasource.getPassword()#">
      SELECT ID, firstName, lastName, username, password,
      emailAddress
      FROM tbl_Users
      WHERE ID = <cfqueryparam cfsqltype="cf_sql_integer"
      value="#arguments.userID#" />
    </cfquery>
  <cfif qSearch.RecordCount>
    <!---If a record has been returned for the userID, create an
      instance of the User bean, and return it.--->
    <cfset objPerson = createObject('component',
      'com.packtApp.oop.beans.User').init(
      ID = qSearch.ID, firstName = qSearch.firstName,
```

```
        lastName = qSearch.lastName, username = qSearch.username,
        password = qSearch.password, emailAddress =
        qSearch.emailAddress) />
     </cfif>
   <cfreturn objPerson />
</cffunction>
```

Listing 5.7 – The `getUserByID()` method

You can see from the code listing that we are sending in a required argument, which is the ID of the User we wish to pull out information for.

Handling select results

To handle returned data from the query, a `cfif` statement is included, to check for the existence of data:

```
<cfif qSearch.RecordCount>
  <!---If a record has been returned for the userID,
     create an instance of the User bean, and return it.--->
  <cfset objPerson = createObject('component',
    'com.packtApp.oop.beans.User').init(
    ID = qSearch.ID, firstName = qSearch.firstName,
    lastName = qSearch.lastName, username = qSearch.username,
    password = qSearch.password,
    emailAddress = qSearch.emailAddress) />
</cfif>
```

Listing 5.8 – A closer look at creating the User bean

If the query result does contain at least one record, the method creates a new User Bean instance and runs the `init()` method, passing the values from the query into the constructor to populate the Bean straight away. We then return the populated User object for use within the application. If no records match the user ID we are requesting, the method will return an empty string.

Listing 5.9 contains the example code to obtain a User bean populated with data from the database.

```
<!--- Instantiate the Datasource object. --->
<cfset objDatasource =
    createObject('component',
    'com.packtApp.oop.beans.Datasource')
    .init(
      DSName='CFOOP',
      username='<your dsn username>',
      password='<your dsn password>'
```

```
    ) />
<!---Instantiate the UserDAO object, and pass in the
  Datasource object.--->
<cfset objUserDAO = createObject('component',
  'com.packtApp.oop.dataAccess.UserDAO').init(
  datasource=objDataSource) />
<!---Obtain the User Bean from the getUserByID() method.--->
<cfset objUserBean = objUserDAO.getUserByID(1) />
<!--- Dump the User Bean.--->
<cfdump var="#objUserBean#" label="Returned User Bean" />
```

Listing 5.9 – Populating a User bean from the datasource

The resulting output from a call to the UserDAO read method using this code sample would look like this, returning a populated User bean ready for use within the application:

The update method

The next function to add from our group of CRUD functions is an update method.

Syntactically, the update function is another relatively simple one to develop and understand. The core of the function, the SQL statement itself, is nothing more than an UPDATE statement, setting new values to the table columns.

Add the following code to the UserDAO.cfc file to include the new method, updateUser():

```
<!--- UPDATE --->
<cffunction name="updateUser" access="public" output="false"
  hint="I update a user's details.">
  <cfargument name="user" required="true"
    type="com.packtApp.oop.beans.User" hint="I am the User bean." />
```

```
            <cfset var qUpdate = '' />
            <cfset var boolSuccess  = true />
              <cftry>
                <cfquery name="qUpdate"
                  datasource="#variables.instance.datasource.getDSName()#"
                  username="#variables.instance.datasource.getUsername()#"
                  password="#variables.instance.datasource.getPassword()#">
                  UPDATE tbl_Users
                  SET firstName = <cfqueryparam cfsqltype="cf_sql_varchar"
                  value="#arguments.user.getFirstName()#" />,
                  lastName     = <cfqueryparam cfsqltype="cf_sql_varchar"
                  value="#arguments.user.getLastName()#" />,
                  username    = <cfqueryparam cfsqltype="cf_sql_varchar"
                  value="#arguments.user.getUsername()#" />,
                  password = <cfqueryparam cfsqltype="cf_sql_varchar"
                  value="#arguments.user.getPassword()#" />,
                  emailAddress  = <cfqueryparam cfsqltype="cf_sql_varchar"
                  value="#arguments.user.getEmailAddress()#" />
                  WHERE
                    ID  = <cfqueryparam cfsqltype="cf_sql_integer"
                    value="#arguments.user.getID()#" />
                </cfquery>
                <cfcatch type="database">
                  <cfset boolSuccess = false />
                </cfcatch>
              </cftry>
        <cfreturn boolSuccess  />
    </cffunction>
```

Listing 5.10 – The `updateUser()` method

You may notice first off that like the `createNewUser()` method, we are sending in the User bean as the required parameter. The User bean itself is populated with the details of the user we wish to update within the database.

The method itself does not return a User bean or any recordset information from the database. In this instance, the function returns a Boolean value. This is set to true by default at the top of the method, and will return true, unless any database errors are caught within the `cftry`/`cfcatch` tags, which will then set the value of the Boolean to false.

Let's create another simple real-world demonstration of this code in use.

We will create a simple form that holds basic information on a user. Once submitted, the form will update the database and return a new User bean, populated with the revised information fresh from the datasource.

Create a new file called `editUser.cfm`, and add the following code to build the form and instantiate the core objects:

```
<h3>Current User Information</h3>
<!--- Instantiate the Datasource object. --->
<cfset objDatasource =
    createObject('component',
    'com.packtApp.oop.beans.Datasource')
    .init(
      DSName='CFOOP',
      username='<your dsn username>',
      password='<your dsn password>'
    ) />


<!---Instantiate the UserDAO object, and pass in the
  Datasource object.--->
<cfset objUserDAO = createObject('component',
  'com.packtApp.oop.dataAccess.UserDAO').init(
  datasource=objDataSource) />


<!---Get the User bean for this user from the DAO.--->
<cfset objUserBean = objUserDAO.getUserByID(7) />
<!---Dump the User Bean so we can see the data it
  currently holds.--->
<cfdump var="#objUserBean#" label="User Bean" />


<!---Check to see if the form has been submitted.--->
<cfif structKeyExists(FORM, 'editUser_btn')>
</cfif>
<cfoutput>
<form name="createUser" action="editUser.cfm" method="POST">
  <label    for="firstName">First name:</label>
  <input    type="text" name="firstName"
    value="#objUserBean.getFirstName()#" /><br />
  <label    for="lastName">Surname:</label>
  <input    type="text" name="lastName"
    value="#objUserBean.getLastName()#" /><br />
  <label    for="emailAddress">Email:</label>
  <input    type="text" name="emailAddress"
    value="#objUserBean.getEmailAddress()#" /><br />
  <input    type="submit" name="editUser_btn"
    value="Edit User" />
</form>
</cfoutput>
```

Listing 5.11 – `editUser.cfm`

Similar to the code in our `addNewUser.cfm` example, here we have a very simple form that displays three elements to edit for a user: their first name, last name, and e-mail address.

We are obtaining our user to edit at the top of the template using the `getUserByID()` method, and a `cfdump` tag displays the current properties of the populated User bean.

We are also using the getter/accessor methods for the properties to set the values of the form elements for us to edit.

Let's add the code within the `cfif` tags that handle the revision and amendments to the user information after the form has been submitted.

```
<!---Check to see if the form has been submitted.--->
<cfif structKeyExists(FORM, 'editUser_btn')>
  <h3>Edited User Information</h3>

  <!---Set the values of the form elements into the
    currently populated User bean object.--->
  <cfset objUserBean.setFirstName(FORM.firstName) />
  <cfset objUserBean.setLastName(FORM.lastName) />
  <cfset objUserBean.setEmailAddress(FORM.emailAddress) />

  <!---Pass this User bean into the updateUser() method.--->
  <cfset objUserDAO.updateUser(user=objUserBean) />
  <!--- Just for this example, let's query the database
```

```
   for the userID and pull out the information to make sure it
   matches the amendments we have made.--->
<cfset objUserBean = objUserDAO.getUserByID(7) />
<cfdump var="#objUserBean#" label="Revised New User Bean" />
</cfif>
```

Listing 5.12 – Adding the form handler functionality to `editUser.cfm`

The `updateUser()` method accepts the User bean as the required argument. We already have the bean instantiated in our page (it is providing the information for the form fields, after all).

We are easily able to update the values of this current Bean using its setter/mutator methods, which we do in the code example by setting the `firstName`, `lastName`, and `emailAddress` property values.

We then send our User bean into the `updateUser()` method, which will update the database record for our individual.

Current User Information

User Bean - component com.packtApp.oop.beans.User		
PROPERTIES	ID	7
	firstName	Merv
	lastName	Turbot
	username	magicalMerv
	password	sublimeFish
	emailAddress	merv@fishybiznez.fake
METHODS		

Edited User Information

Revised New User Bean - component com.packtApp.oop.beans.User		
PROPERTIES	ID	7
	firstName	Mervyn
	lastName	Turbot Esquire
	username	magicalMerv
	password	sublimeFish
	emailAddress	mervyn.t@fishybiznez.fake
METHODS		

First name: Mervyn

Surname: Turbot Esquire

Email: mervyn.t@fishybiznez

(Edit User)

To test whether the database update has been a success, we run another `getUserByID()` method to create a new User bean for the same individual we are updating. Dumping this bean onto the page, we can see that the values within the database have been amended with the new information, which is also reflected in the values of the form elements.

The delete method

Finally, to complete our CRUD requirements, let's add a method to deal with deleting individual user records from the datasource.

Add the following code into the `UserDAO.cfc` file:

```
<!--- DELETE --->
<cffunction name="deleteUserByID" access="public" output="false"
  returntype="boolean" hint="I delete a user from the database.">
  <cfargument name="userID" required="true" type="String"
    hint="I am the ID of the user you wish to delete." />
  <cfset var qDelete = '' />
  <cfset var boolSuccess = true />
    <cftry>
      <cfquery name="qUpdate"
        datasource="#variables.instance.datasource.getDSName()#"
        username="#variables.instance.datasource.getUsername()#"
        password="#variables.instance.datasource.getPassword()#">
        DELETE FROM tbl_Users
        WHERE ID = <cfqueryparam cfsqltype="cf_sql_integer"
          value="#arguments.userID#" />
      </cfquery>
      <cfcatch type="database">
        <cfset boolSuccess = false />
      </cfcatch>
    </cftry>
  <cfreturn boolSuccess />
</cffunction>
```

Listing 5.13 – The `deleteUserByID()` method

As we are only deleting one record at a time, the simplest and easiest way to achieve this is to reference the primary key or ID of the record, much in the same way as we accessed an individual record for our `getUserById()` method. As such, we require an ID value be sent through the arguments, which is then used within the SQL statement to delete the correct record.

We are also handling the return from this method in exactly the same way we handle a return from the `updateUser()` method, which is by sending a Boolean value (set to true by default).

```
<!--- Instantiate the Datasource object. --->
<cfset objDatasource = createObject('component',
  'com.packtApp.oop.beans.Datasource').init(
  DSName='CFOOP', username='<your dsn username>',
                  password='<your dsn password>') />

<!---Instantiate the UserDAO object, and pass in the
  Datasource object.--->
<cfset objUserDAO = createObject('component',
  'com.packtApp.oop.dataAccess.UserDAO') .init(
  datasource=objDataSource) />

<!---Delete a specific user from the database.--->
<cfset objUserDAO.deleteUserByID(4) />
```

Listing 5.14 – Deleting a user through the DAO

Listing 5.14 shows a basic example of using the `deleteUserByID()` method to remove a specific record from the database.

An alternative save method

In the Data Access Object, the `createNewUser()` and `updateUser()` methods are incredibly similar. One creates a new record within the database, while the other updates an existing record's details.

Traditionally, the CRUD methods are all you need to complete your DAO code and interaction with the database to return a single record. However, an alternative function can be placed within the `UserDAO.cfc`, which will effectively handle both the `createNewUser()` and `updateUser()` transactions. The `saveUser()` method will determine which action to take (create or update) based upon results from the second function we will add: the `exists()` method.

Let's create the two new methods within the `UserDAO.cfc` file, beneath the existing CRUD functions.

The save method

We can use the `saveUser()` method whenever we need to either create or update a record within the database. As this method essentially acts as a handler for either the create or update functions, both of which require the User bean as a parameter, the `saveUser()` method also requires the User object.

```
<!--- SAVE --->
<cffunction name="saveUser" access="public" output="false"
  returntype="string" hint="I handle saving a User, either by
  creating a new entry or updating an existing one.">
  <cfargument name="user" required="true"
    type="com.packtApp.oop.beans.User" hint="I am the User bean." />
  <cfset var success = '' />
    <cfif exists(arguments.user)>
      <cfset success = updateUser(arguments.user) />
    <cfelse>
      <cfset success = createNewUser(arguments.user) />
    </cfif>
  <cfreturn success />
</cffunction>
```

Listing 5.15 – The `saveUser()` method

At the top of the function, we set a locally scoped variable called `success` that will hold a default empty string value, which will be updated with the return value of whichever method is used internally.

The line to note within the `saveUser()` method is highlighted in the previous code. The values within the User object are sent to the second function, the `exists()` method. This uses the individual ID key value from the Bean, and runs a query against the database to find any records that have a matching ID value.

If a record does exist, the `updateUser()` method will run, sending through the required User object as an argument within the function.

If there is no match, the record needs to be created, and so the `createNewUser()` method is run.

The exists method

The `saveUser()` method is in place, so we now need to add the `exists()` method to run the database query to check for an existing record.

```
<!--- EXISTS --->
<cffunction name="exists" access="public" output="false"
  returntype="boolean" hint="I check to see if a specific User
  exists within the database, using the ID as a check.">
  <cfargument name="user" required="true"
    type="com.packtApp.oop.beans.User" hint="I am the User
    bean." />
    <cfset var qExists = "">
      <cfquery name="qExists"
        datasource=
```

```
      "#variables.instance.datasource.getDSName()#"
    username=
      "#variables.instance.datasource.getUsername()#"
    password=
      "#variables.instance.datasource.getPassword()#"
    maxrows="1">
      SELECT count(1) as idexists
      FROM tbl_Users
      WHERE ID = <cfqueryparam
        value="#arguments.user.getID()#"
        CFSQLType="cf_sql_integer" />
  </cfquery>
    <cfif qExists.idexists>
      <cfreturn true />
    <cfelse>
      <cfreturn false />
    </cfif>
</cffunction>
```

Listing 5.16 – The `exists()` method

Sending in the User object as the required argument, the `cfquery` tag runs a `SELECT` statement with a SQL `count()` function to ascertain if the record exists.

The `cfquery` tag has the added `maxrows="1"` attribute to ensure only one row is ever returned, and the ID value is drawn from the `getID()` method within the User object.

> You could amend the DAO code further by ensuring that only the `save()` method is available for public use from any `.cfm` template by setting the `access=""` attributes of the `createNewUser()` and `updateUser()` methods to `private`.

After the addition of the new `exists()` and `saveUser()` methods to the `UserDAO` object, our UML diagram of the object would now look like this:

UserDAO
-createNewUser(user:User)
+getUserByID(id:Integer)
-updateUser(user:User)
+deleteUserByID(id:Integer)
+saveUser(user:User)
-exists(user:User)

You can instantly see from the UML that the createNewUser() and updateUser() methods were set to private access to allow the saveUser() method to control the management of the user additions and amendments.

Caching the Data Access Objects

As we have seen, typically Data Access Objects are singleton objects; it only needs to be created once and cached. This is a simple case of assigning the component (or the variable containing the component reference) to a variable in a memory scope, the most common of which are the Session and Application scopes.

The Application scope is ideal for application-specific components, such as Data Access Objects, whereas the Session scope is perfectly suited for holding components and objects relating to a specific user–a shopping cart or User object, for example.

[By caching a component, you have access to all of its properties for as long as the component exists in memory.]

We can add the UserDAO to the Application scope to ensure we have access to the CRUD methods throughout the entire application by adding something similar to the following code within the onApplicationStart() method of your Application.cfc:

```
<cffunction name="onApplicationStart" output="false">
  <!--- Instantiate the Datasource object. --->
    <cfset var objDatasource = createObject('component',
      'com.packtApp.oop.beans.Datasource').init(
        DSName='CFOOP', username='<your dsn username>',
        password='<your dsn password>') />

  <!--- Instantiate the UserDAO object. --->
    <cfset var objUserDAO = createObject('component',
      'com.packtApp.oop.dataAccess.UserDAO').init(
        datasource=objDataSource) />

  <!--- Store the UserDAO in the Application scope. --->
    <cfset Application.userDAO = objUserDAO />
</cffunction>
```

Listing 5.17 – Caching the DAO in the Application scope

The UserDAO is now available on every page inside the application without having to create a new instance of it every time. This method of caching objects is perfect for storing components whose values do not change, such as Data Access Objects.

Dependency Injection

We have seen earlier in this chapter that we were sending a Datasource object into the constructor method of our UserDAO object, to provide the connection details for the datasource.

This is an object-oriented programming technique used to provide information to a specific object for it to work with.

Essentially, **Dependency Injection (DI)** controls what information an object has access to, and therefore, what information it has to work with. Traditionally in procedural programming, an object may have access to information from a variety of sources, and the object itself may have the ability to access and digest this information as needed.

Using Dependency Injection in your object-oriented programming is a highly effective way to control this information; the technique is also known as **Inversion of Control (IoC)**.

This means that the control over what your object receives is inverted and instead of grabbing whatever it needs, the object is provided or fed only the information or data it is allowed to use. As a result it only uses that information it has been given.

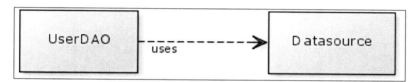

Displaying Dependency Injection using the UML guidelines is incredibly simple. To emphasize a dependency between objects, we join them using a dotted line with an arrowhead, as shown in the previous image.

For a more detailed look into the technique of Dependency Injection, please visit the following wiki site:

http://www.objectorientedcoldfusion.org/wiki/Dependency_Injection.

Summary

In this chapter, we have created a Data Access Object to interact with our database to obtain one record at any time. We have also seen how the DAO works seamlessly with our User bean object to create and read information.

Other topics we have covered in this chapter are:

- The CRUD methods (Create, Read, Update, and Delete)
- Passing Beans as an argument into the DAO
- An introduction to Dependency Injection
- Caching the objects in memory scopes

6
Gateways

In *Chapter 5*, we explored and developed Data Access Objects (DAOs) for our application that managed single-record transactions—one row of data inserted, updated, deleted, or returned at any one time—and how the Bean object was used as the blueprint to hold and manage the values returned from the DAO queries.

Having dealt with these single-record transactions, we now need to focus on reading and handling results from a database query or data provider that returns multiple records per transaction.

Managing an application that may hold and use large amounts of content from a data provider can be a daunting task at times.

It is not uncommon for applications to feature large search interfaces, perhaps with pagination, such as lists of users within a contact application, for example.

When developing object-oriented applications, the burden of dealing with large queries such as these can be easily managed by wrapping all relevant code into one object, a **Gateway**.

In this chapter, we will discuss what a Gateway is and how it can be implemented into your ColdFusion application.

We will also discover:

- The underlying similarities between the Gateway and the Data Access Objects
- Additional benefits of code separation

What is a Gateway?

Sounding mysteriously like a doorway to a mysterious netherworld, a Gateway forms an important part of object-oriented development.

An official description of a Gateway was provided by Martin Fowler, an expert in OOP:

> *A Gateway is an object that encapsulates access to an external system or resource –*
> *Martin Fowler.*

This description states that a Gateway object manages and handles access to

Essentially, this means that a Gateway object will manage and handle access between an application and a data provider, which could be anything such as a relational database, or an external **Application Programming Interface** (**API**) returning XML or JSON formatted data.

Regardless of where the data originates from, or in which format it is returned, the main purpose of the Gateway is to encapsulate the relationship and return the data cleanly and easily back to the application.

Other objects are able to access the resource by sending requests through the Gateway object that returns the data in a format specified by the developer, which can then be easily digested by the object(s) making the initial request.

Working on the same principle as all other objects, if the external API or relational database changes, you only need to make amendments to the particular objects that reference the data source.

A typical ColdFusion Gateway

As our introduction into Gateway objects, we will create an object that will allow us to query our database table of users to retrieve a large query of all records stored, as well as methods that will allow us to search or 'filter' the data to return specific records based upon criteria, suitable for a search interface.

Firstly, let's create a new ColdFusion template file and save it with the name listUsers.cfm. This page will form part of our user management application, and will list all Users currently stored within the database.

Let's add the following code into the listUsers.cfm file:

```
<cfquery name="qlistUsers" datasource="CFOOP" username="<username>"
    password="<password>">
  SELECT ID, firstName, lastName, username, password, emailAddress
```

```
      FROM tbl_Users ORDER BY firstName
</cfquery>
<cfdump var="#qlistUsers#" label="qlistUsers" />
<h3>List All Users</h3>
<ul>
  <cfoutput query="qlistUsers">
    <li><a href="editUser.cfm?ID=#ID#">
      #firstName# #lastName#</a>
    </li>
  </cfoutput>
</ul>
```

Listing 6.1 - `listUsers.cfm`

The code in Listing 6.1 is relatively straightforward; the SQL statement and the query are pulling out all records for all users within the database. We are then looping through the data and adding each line to an unordered list.

We are also wrapping an HTML link element around the user's name, which points to the `editUser.cfm` file, sending with it the ID of the specific database record.

qlistUsers - query						
RESULTSET	**qlistUsers - query**					
		EMAILADDRESS	FIRSTNAME	ID	LASTNAME	PASSWORD	USERNAME
	1	g.brown@flyingcar.com	Gary	6	Brown	flyingCar	gazzaB
	2	matt.j@onenight.fake	Matt	8	James	conf1d3nc3	mattJ
	3	merv.t@fishybiznez.fake	Merv	5	Turbot	sublimeFish	magicalMerv
	4	pete.s@fishybiznez.fake	Pete	3	Sturgeon	sturgywurgy	fishyPete
CACHED	false					
EXECUTIONTIME	1					
SQL	SELECT ID, firstName, lastName, username, password, emailAddress FROM tbl_Users ORDER BY firstName					

List All Users

- Gary Brown
- Matt James
- Merv Turbot
- Pete Sturgeon

The generated output of the code in Listing 6.1 can be seen in the previous screenshot. The output is ideal for the basic requirements. The link over the project name would allow us to create a ColdFusion page to view details on the specific user and edit/update them using the methods within our `UserDAO` object, created in *Chapter 5*.

The `qListUsers` query is returning a recordset that can contain more than one record from the database. Unlike the Data Access Objects in *Chapter 5* which tend to deal specifically with one record at a time, we can use the Gateway object to interact with the datasource and return large queries containing multiple records.

In its current state, the code is too procedural and the query is contained inline on the `listUsers.cfm` template. This is also quite a generic query, returning all users within the database, and could potentially be used in more than one place throughout the application.

Creating a Gateway object

The basic structure of the Gateway object is no different to any other ColdFusion Component we have written so far, wrapped in the `cfcomponent` tag and containing a constructor method.

If we look at a UML diagram of the Gateway object we will initially be creating, we can clearly see that it also contains two methods, `getAllUsers()` and `filterbylastName()`, both of which will return a query object.

```
┌─────────────────────────────────────────┐
│              UserGateway                 │
├─────────────────────────────────────────┤
│          + init():UserGateway            │
│           + getAllUsers()                │
├─────────────────────────────────────────┤
│ + filterByLastName(lastNameFilter:String)│
└─────────────────────────────────────────┘
```

Naming conventions

As far as naming conventions go for the methods themselves, the developer has the freedom to call the methods anything at all, although ideally naming them something relevant to their purpose and function.

Typically, Gateway methods are named as `getAll_x()` of `filter_x()` where x is the descriptive part of the method name, as essentially they are either returning a complete query containing all records, or are running some form of search operation, thereby filtering content using a WHERE clause in the SQL syntax.

Create a new file called `UserGateway.cfc` in the following directory from your webroot: `'com.packtApp.oop.dataAccess.UserGatweay.cfc'`, and copy the following code into the file:

```
<cfcomponent displayname="UserGateway" output="false"
   hint="I am the UserGateway Class.">
   <!--- Pseudo-constructor --->
```

```
<cfset variables.instance = {
  datasource  = ''
} />
<cffunction name="init" access="public" output="false"
  returntype="any" hint="I am the constructor method for
  the UserGateway Class.">
  <cfargument name="datasource" required="true"
    type="com.packtApp.oop.beans.Datasource"
    hint="I am the datasource object." />
  <!--- Set the initial values of the property --->
  <cfscript>
    variables.instance.datasource = arguments.datasource;
  </cfscript>
  <cfreturn this />
</cffunction>
<!--- PUBLIC METHODS --->
</cfcomponent>
```

Listing 6.2 shows the basis for our UserGateway.cfc

Identical to the constructor method used in our Data Access Object, the init()
constructor method accepts a single required argument, datasource, which is the
Datasource bean object, populated with the relevant details to access our database.

```
<!--- Instantiate the Datasource object. --->
<cfset objDatasource = createObject('component',
  'com.packtApp.oop.beans.Datasource').init(
  DSName='CFOOP', username='<username>', password='<password>') />

<!---Instantiate the UserGateway object, and pass in the
  Datasource object.--->
<cfset objUserGW = createObject('component',
  'com.packtApp.oop.dataAccess.UserGateway').init(
  datasource=objDataSource) />
```

Listing 6.3 – Instantiating the UserGateway object

Upon instantiation of the Gateway object, the value of the datasource argument is
stored within the CFCs Variables scope, for use throughout the entire object.

Adding gateway methods

Let's now add the two query functions into our `UserGateway` object, starting with the `getAllUsers()` method, which will return all records within the database table without any filters applied.

Add the following code into the `UserGateway.cfc` file underneath the constructor method:

```
<!--- PUBLIC METHODS --->
<cffunction name="getAllUsers" access="public" output="false"
  hint="I run a query of all users within the database table.">
  <cfset var qAllUsers   = '' />
    <cfquery name="qAllUsers"
      datasource="#variables.instance.datasource.getDSName()#"
      username="#variables.instance.datasource.getUsername()#"
      password="#variables.instance.datasource.getPassword()#">
      SELECT ID, firstName, lastName, username, password,
        emailAddress
      FROM tbl_Users
    </cfquery>
  <cfreturn qAllUsers />
</cffunction>
```

Listing 6.4 – the `getAllUsers()` method

Here in Listing 6.4, you can now see the addition of the `getAllUsers()` method. This query essentially takes the `qlistUsers` query that was seen in Listing 6.1 and places it within the Gateway object.

As seen in *Chapter 5*, in this code we are again reading the properties from the Datasource bean to populate the attributes of our `cfquery` tag, and then we are running a SQL SELECT statement on the entire `tbl_Users` database table.

```
<!--- Instantiate the Datasource object. --->
<cfset objDatasource = createObject('component',
  'com.packtApp.oop.beans.Datasource').init(
  DSName='CFOOP', username='<username>', password='<password>') />

<!---Instantiate the UserGateway object, and pass in the
  Datasource object.--->
<cfset objUserGW = createObject('component',
  'com.packtApp.oop.dataAccess.UserGateway').init(
  datasource=objDataSource) />

<!---Pull out all users within the database.--->
<cfset qResults = objUserGW.getAllUsers() />
```

```
<!---Dump the results.--->
<cfdump var="#qResults#" label="getAllUsers Results" />
```

Listing 6.5 – Getting all users

The code in Listing 6.5, is a brief example of using the `getAllUsers()` method to return a complete query object of all records within the database table, the results of which can be seen as follows:

getAllUsers Results - query							
RESULTSET	**getAllUsers Results - query**						
		EMAILADDRESS	FIRSTNAME	ID	LASTNAME	PASSWORD	USERNAME
	1	g.brown@flyingcar.com	Gary	6	Brown	flyingCar	gazzaB
	2	pete.s@fishybiznez.fake	Pete	3	Sturgeon	sturgywurgy	fishyPete
	3	merv.t@fishybiznez.fake	Merv	5	Turbot	sublimeFish	magicalMerv
	4	matt.j@onenight.fake	Matt	8	James	conf1d3nc3	mattJ
CACHED	false						
EXECUTIONTIME	1						
SQL	SELECT ID, firstName, lastName, username, password, emailAddress FROM tbl_Users						

Let's now add our second gateway function into the object. This method will perform a similar operation to the `getAllUsers()` method by querying the entire database table with the exception of a required argument, which will be used to filter the results based upon the last name of the user.

Add the following code into the `UserGateway.cfc` beneath the `getUsers()` method:

```
<cffunction name="filterByLastName" access="public" output="false"
  hint="I run a query of all users within the database table based
  upon a required filter.">
  <cfargument name="lastNameFilter" required="true" type="String"
    hint="I am the filter you wish to apply for the last name of the
    user." />
  <cfset var qUserFilter   = '' />
    <cfquery name="qUserFilter"
      datasource="#variables.instance.datasource.getDSName()#"
      username="#variables.instance.datasource.getUsername()#"
      password="#variables.instance.datasource.getPassword()#">
      SELECT ID, firstName, lastName, username, password,
        emailAddress
      FROM tbl_Users
      WHERE
        lastName LIKE
        <cfqueryparam cfsqltype="cf_sql_varchar"
          value="#arguments.lastNameFilter#" />
    </cfquery>
```

```
        <cfreturn qUserFilter />
    </cffunction>
```

Listing 6.6 – the `filterByLastName()` method

Incredibly similar to the `getAllUsers()` method, in Listing 6.6 you can see the SQL statement has been amended to include a WHERE clause, which will filter the query results based upon the value sent through in the `arguments` scope.

```
<!--- Instantiate the Datasource object. --->
<cfset objDatasource = createObject('component',
    'com.packtApp.oop.beans.Datasource').init(
    DSName='CFOOP', username='<username>', password='<password>') />

<!---Instantiate the UserGateway object, and pass in the
    Datasource object.--->
<cfset objUserGW = createObject('component',
    'com.packtApp.oop.dataAccess.UserGateway').init(
    datasource=objDataSource) />

<!---Filter a user to obtain results. We can use wildcard
    operators as well.--->
<cfset qResults = objUserGW.filterByLastName('%tu%') />

<!---Dump the results.--->
<cfdump var="#qResults#" label="filterByLastName Results" />
```

Listing 6.7 – Search for a user using a filter

Code Listing 6.7 shows a basic example of using the `filterByLastName()` method to return a query of records from the database. Here we are sending in a specific text string wrapped in wildcard operators as the required argument, and using that value to perform the LIKE comparison in the SQL WHERE clause.

filterByLastName Results - query		
RESULTSET	filterByLastName Results - query	
		EMAILADDRESS	FIRSTNAME	ID	LASTNAME	PASSWORD	USERNAME
		1	pete.s@fishybiznez.fake	Pete	3	Sturgeon	sturgywurgy	fishyPete
		2	merv.t@fishybiznez.fake	Merv	5	Turbot	sublimeFish	magicalMerv
CACHED	false	
EXECUTIONTIME	1	
SQL	SELECT ID, firstName, lastName, username, password, emailAddress FROM tbl_Users WHERE lastName LIKE ?	
SQLPARAMETERS	filterByLastName Results - array	
	1	%tu%

In the previous screenshot, you can see the results returned from the
`filterbyLastName()` method that match the required filter string passed into
the function.

Minimising code duplication

After adding our two select queries into the `UserGateway` object, we have seen quite
clearly that there are not many differences between the two queries themselves; both
are querying the same columns within the table, both are returning a query object.
The only difference lies with the filter aspect and any arguments sent through into
the `WHERE` clause of the query itself.

At the moment, our `UserGateway` object could probably continue as it is with these
theo methods both containing their own versions of the SQL statement.

Consider, however, what would happen once we started to expand our requirements
by adding in more filter methods. If we continued to supply a SQL statement with
each function, we would not only be creating extra lines in our files that could lead
to something incredibly difficult or frustrating to navigate and debug, but more
importantly we would be unnecessarily duplicating the SQL statement and the
`cfquery` code.

As a rule of thumb, it's normally better to pre-empt this kind of problem and plan
ahead than to have to refactor your code later and amend your components
and objects.

And so, to avoid this situation, we can amend our Gateway object to contain only
one method that will handle all of our multi-record transactions, whether they need
a filter or not.

Revising the gateway object

We will begin by re-writing our `UserGateway.cfc` to include the revised methods. Essentially, we are stripping out every method with the exception of the `init()` constructor method to revert back to the code as shown in Listing 6.2.

Let's once more take a look at the UML diagram for the revised `UserGateway` object.

UserGateway
+init():UserGateway
+ getAllUsers()
+ filterByLastName(lastNameFilter:String)
+ filterByEmailAddress(emailAddress:String)
-filterAllUsers(filter:String)

We will be adding in three methods that will be publicly accessible outside of the CFC, which are clearly visible in the UML diagram thanks to the plus sign (+) prepending each method name.

The fourth method, `filterAllUsers()`, is a private function accessible only within the component itself. It is this method that will contain the actual SQL statement used by the three public functions, which will call this method to obtain the results from the database.

Let's add the three public methods into our revised `UserGateway` object.

```
<!--- PUBLIC METHODS --->
<cffunction name="getAllUsers" access="public" output="false"
  hint="I run a query of all users within the database table.">
  <!---Call the query method and return the query object.--->
  <cfreturn filterAllUsers() />
</cffunction>

<cffunction name="filterByLastName" access="public" output="false"
  hint="I run a query of all users within the database table based
  upon a required filter.">
    <cfargument name="lastNameFilter" required="true" type="string"
      hint="I am the lastname to filter." />
    <!---Create and populate a structure object containing the filter
      to pass through.--->
      <cfset var stuFilter = {
        lastname = arguments.lastNameFilter
      } />
```

```
    <!---Send the structure into the query method and return the
    query object.--->
      <cfreturn filterAllUsers(stuFilter) />
  </cffunction>


  <cffunction name="filterByEmailAddress" access="public"
    output="false" hint="I query the database to find a user
    with a matching email address.">
      <cfargument name="emailAddress" required="true" type="string"
        hint="I am the email address to search for." />
      <!---Create and populate a structure object containing the filter
        to pass through.--->
      <cfset var stuFilter = {
        emailAddress = arguments.emailAddress
      } />

    <!---Send the structure into the query method and return the
    query object.--->
      <cfreturn filterAllUsers(stuFilter) />
  </cffunction>
```

Listing 6.8 – adding our filter methods to the Gateway object

The code in Listing 6.8 shows our three public methods within the Gateway object. Each of these functions calls and directly returns the value of the private method, `filterAllUsers()`.

Two of our methods require a filter argument to amend the SQL statement, and so we create a structure populated with the filter values from their arguments, which is then passed into the `filterAllUsers()` method.

Let's now add the `filterAllUsers()` method, which contains our SQL statement.

```
  <!--- PRIVATE METHODS --->
  <cffunction name="filterAllUsers" access="private" output="false"
    hint="I run a query and will return all user records. If a filter
    has been supplied, I will refine the search using the filter
    information sent to me.">
    <cfargument name="filter" required="false" type="Struct"
      default="#structNew()#" hint="I am a structure used to filter
      the query." />
    <cfset var qSearch = '' />
      <cfquery name="qSearch"
        datasource="#variables.instance.datasource.getDSName()#"
        username="#variables.instance.datasource.getUsername()#"
        password="#variables.instance.datasource.getPassword()#">
```

```
          SELECT ID, firstName, lastName, username, password,
            emailAddress
          FROM tbl_Users
          WHERE 1 = 1
    <cfif NOT structIsEmpty(arguments.filter)>
      <!---A filter has been provided. Let's find out which filter it
        is, and apply the necessary clause to the SQL.--->
      <!--- Perform a LIKE comparison on the lastname --->
      <cfif structKeyExists(arguments.filter, 'lastname')>
        AND lastname LIKE
          <cfqueryparam cfsqltype="cf_sql_varchar"
            value="#arguments.filter.lastname#" />
      </cfif>
      <!--- Here, we want to find exact email address matches. --->
      <cfif structKeyExists(arguments.filter, 'emailAddress')>
        AND emailAddress =
          <cfqueryparam cfsqltype="cf_sql_varchar"
              value="#arguments.filter.emailAddress#" />
      </cfif>
    </cfif>
        </cfquery>
    <cfreturn qSearch />
  </cffunction>
```

Listing 6.9 – adding the core query function to the Gateway object

The code in Listing 6.9 shows the primary database interaction method, which contains the SQL statement to query the database.

This method accepts one parameter, which is a structure containing the filter string. It is this structure value which is then used within the filterAllUsers() method to determine if the SQL statement is amended with the extra filter information.

Although we have drastically amended the contents of the UserGateway object by revising these methods, we have not changed the process of calling the query, and so our existing code in Listings 6.5 and 6.7 would still work. The Gateway pattern ensures that the access to the database was encapsulated and maintained without affecting how the rest of the application functioned and called the methods.

We also went some way to tidy up the contents of the Gateway component to streamline the amount of code involved.

The larger the number of filter methods calling the primary SQL query you wished to include within the Gateway object, the bigger and possibly more confusing the `cfif` statement within the `filterAllUsers()` method may become. You may then run the risk of making your code incredibly difficult or confusing to manage and maintain.

In this instance, perhaps the Gateway would be better suited to contain a separate SQL statement within each function. The choice and option is ultimately down to you as a developer, what will work best for you and the application.

Caching the Gateway object

Incredibly similar in form, function, and purpose as Data Access Objects, Gateway objects are also classed as a singleton object; it only needs to be created once and then cached for use throughout the application.

We can alter the `onApplicationStart()` method in your `Application.cfc` to include the following highlighted code:

```
<cffunction name="onApplicationStart" output="false">
    <!--- Instantiate the Datasource object. --->
      <cfset var objDatasource = createObject('component',
        'com.packtApp.oop.beans.Datasource').init(
          DSName='CFOOP', username='<your dsn username>',
          password='<your dsn password>') />

    <!--- Instantiate the UserDAO object. --->
      <cfset var objUserDAO = createObject('component',
        'com.packtApp.oop.dataAccess.UserDAO').init(
          datasource=objDataSource) />

    <!--- Instantiate the UserGateway object. --->
    <cfset var objUserGW = createObject('component',
      'com.packtApp.oop.dataAccess.UserGateway').init(
      datasource=objDataSource) />

    <!--- Store the UserDAO in the Application scope. --->
      <cfset Application.userDAO = objUserDAO />

    <!--- Store the UserGW in the Application scope. --->
      <cfset Application.userGW = objUserGW />
  </cffunction>
```

Listing 6.10 – Caching the Gateway in the application scope

The `UserGateway` is now available on every page throughout the application as it is stored and persisted within the `Application` scope.

The Gateway discussion

There has been many a strong discussion on the implementation and understanding of Gateways in ColdFusion applications over the years, and there still doesn't seem to be any definitive answer or rule of thumb for the architecture and use of them in a design pattern environment.

Most object-oriented design patterns incorporated into ColdFusion development resemble common design patterns used in J2EE/Java.

We have already discussed Bean objects and Data Access Object in previous chapters, both of which are commonly used in most object-oriented design patterns, across any development language.

The Gateway, however, isn't necessarily a direct copy of the Java OO equivalent. In fact, there seems to be a level of uncertainty over what it actually is.

No hard and fast rules

We have read earlier on in this chapter that a Gateway encapsulates access to an external system or resource, and generally deals with items that are not objects, such as database tables.

Furthermore, by separating the multi-record queries such as getAllUsers() from the single-row queries or the CRUD methods, developers and SQL programmers both have a simplified series of component packages and a firmer understanding of where the methods reside in terms of the code base.

It is for this reason alone that the method of creating a Gateway shown so far in this chapter has been inherited and used by the vast majority of ColdFusion developers over the years.

There is an alternative method of creating and using Gateways inside the design patterns, which stems from the Table Data Gateway.

Table Data Gateway

> *An object that acts as a Gateway to a database table. One instance handles all the rows in the table. — Martin Fowler*

We know that the definition of a Gateway is an object that has "access to an external system or resource". In *"Patterns of Enterprise Application Architecture"*, *Martin Fowler* describes a Table Data Gateway as an object that acts as a Gateway to a database table.

This is an extension of sorts on his previous quote which outlines the fact that there is an 'external resource'. With the new addition of the Table Data Gateway, that external resource has been clarified as a database table.

This marries up nicely with the fact that the Gateway should encapsulate access to the resource.

The definition of the Table Data Gateway continues to say the following:

> *A Table Data Gateway holds all the SQL for accessing a single table or view: selects, inserts, updates, and deletes. Other code calls its methods for all interaction with the database.*

Similarities to Data Access Objects

As we know, Data Access Objects (DAOs) are used to encapsulate access to the datasource, typically dealing with single-row data. However, given that OOP is primarily a concept derived from Java/J2EE programming, an official note on the usage of DAOs provided by Sun Microsystems when referencing the Core J2EE OO Pattern is that the DAO is used to encapsulate all access to the datasource.

 More information on the Core Data Access Object definition can be found here:

```
http://java.sun.com/blueprints/corej2eepatterns/
Patterns/DataAccessObject.html.
```

This would suggest that a viable use of the DAO would be to control every aspect of database access including all queries that deal with multiple results, and not just the standard single-row CRUD methods (create, read, update, and delete).

The solution provided for DAO usability in this case sounds incredibly similar to the typical usage of the Gateway object.

On a similar note, the comparison between the DAO and the Table Data Gateway are incredibly close in terms of purpose, leading to an assumption that the Data Access Object pattern and the Table Data Gateway pattern are theoretically one and the same.

Both objects are designed to encapsulate access to a database table, and both seem to have the definition of handling all access in single- or multi-record form.

The TDG pattern and the DAO pattern are able to deal with not only CRUD methods, but also getAll_x() methods, such as the getAllUsers() function.

Combining the two patterns

An alternative solution would be to combine the two patterns into one object. They both perform the same basic function, and both have the core functionality of dealing with all access to the database.

It would therefore be feasible to create a revised data object which contains all code and methods relating to database access and querying.

There is no set rule on calling this object a Table Data Gateway pattern, either. Personal preference and development practices will define what you feel most comfortable calling an object such as this. You could create a Table Data Gateway object, stay with either a Data Access object or Gateway object, or create your own naming convention.

Whichever option you choose will work for you. In this instance, let's imagine we have created a `UserTDG.cfc` object, which will include all of the methods from our `UserDAO` and `UserGateway` objects.

As such, we could visualize the object by creating a UML diagram to represent its structure, which would look something like this:

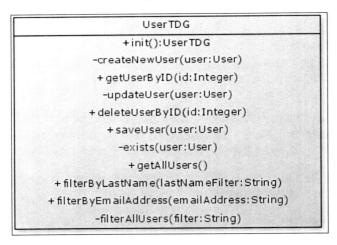

In this object, we have now combined the CRUD methods from our original Data Access Object with the more general `getAll_x()` and `filter_X()` methods from our Gateway.

We still have the `init()` method to instantiate the object, into which we pass the reference to the datasource, as all functions within this object will be accessing the database. Instantiation of the object would not differ from the example shown earlier, and we now only have one object in which to call ANY database-related methods.

Which option is best?

Having read this chapter and seen the similarities between the Gateway and Data Access Objects in their elementary states, and having compared the underlying definitions of each, the fundamental question you may be asking yourself is which option should I use?

Why keep DAOs and Gateways as separate objects if the two seem so similar?

The common answer is that by separating the two objects, you have a way of differentiating between the two forms of database interaction—single-row manipulation, and multi-record retrieval. You know exactly what CFC file contains which set of queries.

The suggestions and definitions outlined in this chapter all relate to Java-based object-oriented programming. Should ColdFusion need to follow the exact patterns and get rid of the separate Gateway object?

Typically, when writing Data Access Object patterns, the single-record SQL statements tend not to change. It is a simple matter of managing one record through the CRUD methods. They are fairly static, and once written need not be amended too many times.

The Gateway methods containing possibly large and detailed SELECT statements (depending on the structure of your relational database tables) may need to be edited, amended, and tweaked fairly regularly as needs and requirements change. This is possibly another reason to keep the methods separate. The Data Access Object can manage its CRUD methods without much need for change, leaving the independent Gateway CFC for the developer to amend without causing any disruption to the other code.

Simply because design patterns are based upon those within the J2EE environment, doesn't mean they must follow the structure and usage 'word for word'.

The rest of the code in this book, and the application samples it builds along the way, uses the method stated at the start of the book—a separate Gateway and Data Access Object component for each package. This is not to say that this is the best method to use—it has simply been implemented this way to easily show the separation between the two objects.

You have the option to use whichever method you feel best suits your applications, and ultimately that you feel most comfortable with.

Summary

In this chapter, we have discussed the use of Gateway patterns in an object-oriented application.

We have gained a deeper understanding of the underlying definition of the Gateway, and have looked in some detail to an alternative solution by merging all database queries and functions into one Data Access Object pattern, or the Table Data Gateway pattern.

7

Creating a Service Layer

Up to this point, our application consists of two packages, one for the projects and another for the users. Both packages contain a Data Access Object, dealing with single-row data transactions; a Gateway object, dealing with multiple-record database transactions; and a Bean object, to contain and persist the informatioln where required.

Beans are transient, due in large to the fact that they are typically persisted across the entire application and can pass through all layers in the tiered architecture.

In this chapter, we will discover the power and abilities of service layers within our application. A structured application built with service objects removes any major issues with object dependency, meaning that, to an extent the objects instantiated within your application are not dependent upon having the knowledge of the inner workings of any other objects and what each one does, but instead they simply need the ability to communicate with each other to perform the actions required.

We will alter our application to no longer create the Data Access Objects or Gateway objects directly, instead choosing to use the Service Layer for direct method calls, which in turn will communicate with the DAOs and Gateways to perform the database enquiries.

We will also look into the following:

- Amending existing code to call the service layer
- Streamlining the CRUD and Gateway methods
- Object inheritance

What is a Service Layer?

A Service Layer is quite an easy object-oriented concept to understand.

Let's run a test scenario.

You're up late. You've been working for hours on end trying to complete some urgent coding amendments that need to be delivered to a tight deadline. You're tired, but my goodness the work is done. You're dedicated—what more can anyone ask for. Be proud.

Just as you finish the final keystroke and save the work, your stomach rumbles. You know what that means. It's time for some food, then off to bed to sleep for an eternity.

Your stomach has told you what to do with the "sleepyStomachRumble()" method. You just need to follow orders now, and you kick into auto-pilot.

First things first, time to shutdown the computer, using the "pcOff()" method. Slide yourself off from your office chair using the "deskEscape()" function, and off to the kitchen to prepare a few slices of toast; "breadIn()", "toasterOn()", and "spreadJam()" methods respectively.

After savoring your hard-earned slices of toast, it's time to turn off the lights and head to bed; "lightsOff()", "quickShower()", and "sleepLikeALog()" methods.

Mission accomplished.

A slightly bizarre situation, I grant you, but in this particular situation you are acting as a Service Layer.

You had the "sleepyStomachRumble()" method pre-built into your psyche—hours of late night development will do that to you—but that one method was coordinating other objects and their contained methods to complete the process to take you away from the desk and into the kitchen for food before whisking you away for a good night's sleep.

In essence, one method was called, an easily memorable method name, but underneath that single method runs a series of other functions to complete the task. No one needs to be exposed to the intricacies or the details. All that needs to be run is the "sleepyStomachRumble()" method.

A Service Layer forms a basic Facade Pattern for the application, and a simple interface to interact with the code base.

Facade patterns in a nutshell

A **Facade Pattern** is a type of design pattern commonly used in object-oriented programming. The word 'facade' stems from the French language, and literally means 'frontage' or 'face', and a facade pattern is an object that provides a simplified interface to a larger body of code, such as a Class package or library.

A facade can:

- Make a component library or group of packages easier to use and understand, since the facade has convenient methods for common tasks
- Make code that uses the library more readable, for the same reason
- Reduce dependencies of outside code on the inner workings of a library, since most code uses the facade, thereby allowing more flexibility in developing the system
- Wrap a collection of APIs with a single well-designed API

Creating a service

A major benefit to creating a service layer is the fact that it creates a simpler, easier interface to interact with and access the data through the larger collection of packages and Class libraries within your code base.

The service layer can also manage the instantiation of related objects.

To highlight the effectiveness of using a Service layer (or Facade Pattern) in your larger applications, the code used in this chapter has grown. We now have not only a component package dealing with User interactions (the Bean, DAO, and Gateway), we also have a package dealing with the user's address, which is available in the complete code download for this chapter.

Let's take a look at the `onApplicatonStart()` method as it currently stands within the `Application.cfc` file.

```
<cffunction name="onApplicationStart" output="false">
  <!--- Instantiate the Datasource object. --->
    <cfset var objDatasource = createObject('component',
      'com.packtApp.oop.beans.Datasource').init(
      DSName='CFOOP', username='<your dsn username>',
      password='<your dsn password>') />
  <!--- Instantiate the UserDAO object. --->
    <cfset var objUserDAO = createObject('component',
      'com.packtApp.oop.dataAccess.UserDAO').init(
      datasource=objDataSource) />
```

```
<!--- Instantiate the UserGateway object. --->
  <cfset var objUserGW = createObject('component',
    'com.packtApp.oop.dataAccess.UserGateway').init(
    datasource=objDataSource) />
<!--- Store the UserDAO in the Application scope. --->
  <cfset Application.userDAO = objUserDAO />
<!--- Store the UserGW in the Application scope. --->
  <cfset Application.userGW = objUserGW />
<!--- Instantiate the AddressDAO object. --->
  <cfset var objAddressDAO = createObject('component',
    'com.packtApp.oop.dataAccess.AddressDAO').init(
    datasource=objDataSource) />
<!--- Instantiate the AddressGateway object. --->
  <cfset var objAddressGW = createObject('component',
    'com.packtApp.oop.dataAccess.AddressGateway').init(
    datasource=objDataSource) />
<!--- Store the addressDAO in the Application scope. --->
  <cfset Application.addressDAO = objAddressDAO />
<!--- Store the addressGW in the Application scope. --->
  <cfset Application.addressGW = objAddressGW />
</cffunction>
```

Listing 7.1 - `Application.cfc` (before services)

Looking at the code in Listing 7.1, there are currently four objects being instantiated and added to the `Application` scope for persistence throughout the application.

All of these objects are directly related to the two packages we have within the code base; the User's package and the Address package respectively, and from each package we are accessing the Gateway and the Data Access Object.

Let's visualize these objects in another UML diagram, being instantiated from the `Application.cfc` file.

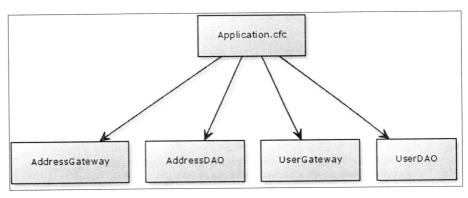

Although this is entirely feasible, we can and should streamline the instantiation of the objects as their dependencies dictate. This will help reduce any 'clutter' from the onApplicationStart() method, and will also help to improve the solidity and structure of our application's underlying model framework.

We will start to enhance our application's code structure even more by creating a Service Layer component for each of the packages.

Defining the User Service

The main purpose of the User Service object is to be a single point of entry for anything that requires access to user functionality, whether it's a Controller, a standard .cfm template page, or a Web Services call.

A service object is no different in terms of basic layout and structure from any of the other ColdFusion components we have written and discussed so far within this book.

Listing 7.2 shows the bare bones structure of the CFC, complete with the init() method used for the instantiation of the object. Create a new file called UserService.cfc within the com/packtApp/oop/dataAccess directory within your application, and add the following code to the file:

```
<cfcomponent displayname="UserService" output="false"
  hint="I am the UserSVC Class used to interact with the
  User package.">

  <!--- Pseudo-constructor --->
  <cfset variables.instance = {
    userDAO = '',
    userGW       = ''
  } />
  <cffunction name="init" access="public" output="false"
    returntype="any" hint="I am the constructor method for
    the UserSVC Class.">
  <cfargument name="datasource" required="true"
    type="com.packtApp.oop.beans.Datasource"
    hint="I am the datasource object." />

    <!--- Set the initial values of the Bean --->
    <cfscript>
    // instantiate the Data Access Object
    variables.instance.userDAO = createObject(
      'component', 'UserDAO' ).init(arguments.datasource);
    // instantiate the Gateway
```

```
        variables.instance.userGW = createObject(
          'component', 'UserGateway').init(arguments.datasource);
      </cfscript>
    <cfreturn this />
    </cffunction>
    <!--- CRUD METHODS --->
    <!--- GATEWAY METHODS --->
  </cfcomponent>
```

Listing 7.2 – `UserService.cfc`

The main purpose of the user service layer is to provide a simpler interface for the developer/client to interact with the detailed packages already developed. The User package needs to access, store, and retrieve information from the database, which is why the Data Access Objects and Gateway components were developed.

Although this works amazingly well, not all of the methods they contain need to be made available for 'public consumption'. For example, we don't need to expose all of the `save()`, `exists()`, or `filterBy_X()` methods. The packages know what methods need to be run when a certain function has been called — the next thing we can do is to simplify the way they are being called.

As we need access to the User DAO and Gateway components, we have included their instantiation within the `init()` method in the User Services layer, passing through the datasource object from the arguments scope as it is a required parameter in both the DAO and Gateway. We are then assigning both of the new objects to an expression within the `variables.instance` structure within the CFC.

The DAO and Gateway objects have been stored within the service component for use throughout the Users package. Although they are two separate objects each containing their own methods and functions, as we have merged them into the service component, all of those methods are available for us to use as though they are part of the original component.

Adding the CRUD methods

The first object instantiated in the `init()` method of the `UserService` component is the `UserDAO` component.

This object, as you will hopefully remember, was developed to deal with the single-row database access. The four main methods within this object dealt with the **CRUD** transactions; Create, Read, Update, and Delete.

We also created two other functions called `save()` and `exists()`. The `save()` method was written as a single entry method that would handle the creation of a new record, or the update of an existing database record by calling the `exists()` method to check if the ID value already existed in the database. If so, an update was performed on that row of data, if not, a new record was inserted into the database.

At this stage in development, we had already helped to streamline code and optimize the function calls by providing the ability to run one of the two database functions by only calling one method, the `save()` method.

Although the DAO contains six methods in total (not including the `init()` constructor method), we need to reference only three of them within the service layer for the users package, as it is only these three that need to be publicly accessible.

Let's add the following three functions shown in Listing 7.3 to the `UserService.cfc` file to add more functionality to our user package API.

```
<!--- CRUD METHODS --->
<cffunction name="save" access="public" output="false"
  hint="I save or update a User into the database.">
  <cfargument name="user" required="true"
  type="com.packtApp.oop.beans.User" hint="I am the User bean." />
  <cfreturn variables.instance.userDAO.saveUser(arguments.user) />
</cffunction>
<cffunction name="read" access="public" output="false"
  hint="I obtain details for a specific User from the database.">
  <cfargument name="userID" required="true" type="numeric"
    hint="I am the ID of the user you wish to search for." />
  <cfreturn variables.instance.userDAO.getUserByID(arguments.userID)
  />
</cffunction>
<cffunction name="delete" access="public" output="false"
  hint="I delete a specific User the database.">
  <cfargument name="userID" required="true" type="String"
    hint="I am the ID of the user you wish to delete." />
  <cfreturn
    variables.instance.userDAO.deleteUserByID(arguments.userID)/>
</cffunction>
```

Listing 7.3 - `UserService.cfc` (CRUD method callers)

Our three methods, `save()`, `read()`, and `delete()` have now been placed inside the service component.

All of the SQL and database transactions have already been written within the DAO itself. We do not want to duplicate any code—we have no requirement to. As the DAO has been stored within the service component, we simply need to call the relevant function within the object to run its method, `variables.instance.userDao.save()` for example.

Listing 7.4 shows a clearer breakdown of the `save()` method from the projects service layer:

```
<cffunction name="save" access="public" output="false"
  hint="I save or update a User into the database.">
  <!--- send in the required user object --->
  <cfargument name="user" required="true"
    type="com.packtApp.oop.beans.User" hint="I am the User bean." />
  <!--- call the save() method within the userDAO --->
  <cfreturn variables.instance.userDAO.saveUser(arguments.user) />
</cffunction>
```

Listing 7.4 – breakdown of the `save()` method

Adding the Gateway methods

In the same way we have added the functions from the User package Data Access Object, we now need to add the functions from the Gateway object, as show in Listing 7.5.

```
<!--- GATEWAY METHODS --->
<cffunction name="getAllUsers" access="public" output="false"
  hint="I run a query of all users within the database table.">

  <!--- Call the query method from the User Gateway and return the
    query object. --->
  <cfreturn variables.instance.userGW.filterAllUsers() />
</cffunction>
<cffunction name="filterByLastName" access="public" output="false"
  hint="I run a query of all users within the database
  table based upon a required filter.">
    <cfargument name="lastNameFilter" required="true" type="string"
      hint="I am the lastname to filter." />

  <!--- Create and populate a structure object containing the filter
    to pass through. --->
    <cfset var stuFilter = {
      lastname = arguments.lastNameFilter
    } />
```

```
<!--- Send the structure into the query method and
   return the query object. --->
   <cfreturn variables.instance.userGW.filterAllUsers(stuFilter) />
</cffunction>
<cffunction name="filterByEmailAddress" access="public"
   output="false" hint="I query the database to find a user
   with a matching email address.">
   <cfargument name="emailAddress" required="true" type="string"
      hint="I am the email address to search for." />

   <!--- Create and populate a structure object containing the filter
      to pass through. --->
      <cfset var stuFilter = {
         emailAddress = arguments.emailAddress
      } />

   <!--- Send the structure into the query method and
      return the query object. --->
      <cfreturn variables.instance.userGW.filterAllUsers(stuFilter) />
</cffunction>
```

Listing 7.5 - `UserService.cfc` (Gateway method callers)

Again, the methods are in place, but no SQL or database transactions are in sight. We have already written those, and have no desire to write them again. We want to keep all database calls and SQL statements locked to the DAO and Gateway objects only. This way, we only have the two files in which to change the relevant SQL if required.

The purpose of the service layer is to provide a simple interface to call the previously developed and detailed methods.

As in the previous example, once a function is called within the `UserService` component, the relevant method is called from the User Gateway object:

```
<cffunction name="getAllUsers" access="public" output="false"
   hint="I run a query of all users within the database table.">
   <!--- Call the query method from the User Gateway and return the
      query object. --->
   <cfreturn variables.instance.userGW.filterAllUsers() />
</cffunction>
```

Listing 7.6 – breakdown of the `filterByParent()` method

Adding an abstract class

We can further extend the functions available within the UserService object by adding a base class to the component to aid in code reuse.

We have the coreUtils.cfc component (com/packtApp/oop/utils/coreUtils.cfc), which we can use to contain generic methods and functions that we can share across all of our components if necessary. Let's add a new function to this abstract class, which will allow us to view the values of the variables.instance structure within the object we call it from:

```
<cfcomponent displayname="coreUtils" output="false"
  hint="I am the coreUtils abstract Class.">
  <cffunction name="getMemento" access="public" output="false"
    hint="I return the variables.instance struct.">
  <cfreturn variables.instance />
  </cffunction>
</cfcomponent>
```

Listing 7.7 – com/utils/core.cfc (adding getMemento() method)

To complete this step, we next need to amend the UserService component and add the extends="" attribute to point to the coreUtils.cfc abstract class:

```
<cfcomponent displayname="UserSVC" output="false"
    hint="I am the UserSVC Class used to interact with the
    User package." extends="com.packtApp.oop.utils.coreUtils">
```

Listing 7.8 - UserService.cfc (adding the extends attribute)

In Listing 7.8, we have added the path to the coreUtils.cfc file in the extends attribute within the cfcomponent tag.

```
<cfdump var="#Application.userSVC.getMemento()#" />
```

Listing 7.9 – calling the getMemento() function

The following screenshot shows the dumped values of the code in Listing 7.9, which returns the variables.instance structure within the User Service object:

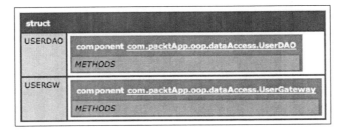

The following UML diagram shows the `UserService` object and the inheritance connection with the `coreUtils` component.

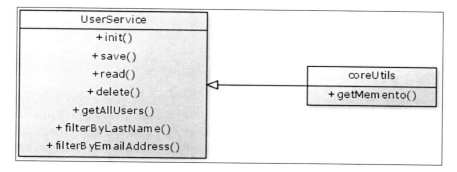

Defining the address service

Let's repeat the process for the second of our packages used within the application, the user package.

Create a new file called `AddressService.cfc` within the `com/packtApp/oop/dataAccess` directory within your application, and add the following code to the file:

```
<cfcomponent displayname="AddressSVC" output="false"
  hint="I am the AddressSVC Class used to interact
  with the Address package.">

  <!--- Pseudo-constructor --->
  <cfset variables.instance = {
    addressDAO = '',
    addressGW = ''
  } />
  <cffunction name="init" access="public" output="false"
    returntype="any" hint="I am the constructor method for
    the AddressSVC Class.">
  <cfargument name="datasource" required="true"
    type="com.packtApp.oop.beans.Datasource" hint="I am the
    datasource object." />
    <!--- Set the initial values of the Bean --->
    <cfscript>
    // instantiate the Data Access Object
    variables.instance.addressDAO = createObject(
      'component', 'AddressDAO').init(arguments.datasource);
    // instantiate the Gateway
    variables.instance.addressGW = createObject(
      'component', 'AddressGateway').init(arguments.datasource);
```

```
      </cfscript>
    <cfreturn this />
    </cffunction>
    <!--- CRUD METHODS --->
    <!--- GATEWAY METHODS --->
  </cfcomponent>
```

Listing 7.10 – `com/packtApp/oop/dataAccess/AddressService.cfc`

As in the previous example, we first define the basic structure for the ColdFusion component, and add the constructor method to instantiate the object. We also send through the datasource name as a required parameter, and create the user package Data Access Object and Gateway object, again storing them in the `variables.instance` structure within the service layer.

Notice in Listing 7.10, we have already defined the path to the `coreUtils.cfc` within the `extends` attribute, thereby inheriting the functions from the abstract class for use within this object.

We next need to add the DAO methods into the service object to interact with the functions in the users Data Access Object.

```
<cffunction name="save" access="public" output="false"
  hint="I save or update an Address into the database.">
  <cfargument name="address" required="true"
    type="com.packtApp.oop.beans.Address"
    hint="I am the Address bean." />
  <cfreturn
    variables.instance.addressDAO.saveAddress(arguments.address) />
</cffunction>
<cffunction name="read" access="public" output="false"
  hint="I obtain details for a specific address from the database.">
  <cfargument name="ID" required="true" type="numeric"
    hint="I am the ID of the address you wish to search for." />
  <cfreturn
    variables.instance.addressDAO.getAddressByID(arguments.ID) />
</cffunction>
<cffunction name="delete" access="public" output="false"
  hint="I delete a specific Address the database.">
  <cfargument name="ID" required="true" type="String"
    hint="I am the ID of the address you wish to delete." />
  <cfreturn
    variables.instance.addressDAO.deleteAddressByID(arguments.ID) />
</cffunction>
```

Listing 7.11 – `AddressService.cfc` (CRUD method callers)

Finally, we need to add the Gateway method callers into the `AddressService` component to interact with the Gateway object and run the multiple record data transactions against the database, as in Listing 7.12.

```
<!--- GATEWAY METHODS --->
<cffunction name="getAllAddresses" access="public" output="false"
  hint="I run a query of all users within the database table.">

<!--- Call the query method and return the query object. --->
  <cfreturn variables.instance.addressGW.getAllAddresses() />
</cffunction>
<cffunction name="filterByUserID" access="public" output="false"
  hint="I run a query of all addresses within the database
  table based upon a required filter.">
    <cfargument name="userID" required="true" type="string"
      hint="I am the userID to filter." />

  <!--- Create and populate a structure object containing the
    filter to pass through. --->
    <cfset var stuFilter = {
      userID = arguments.userID
    } />
  <!--- Send the structure into the query method and
    return the query object. --->
    <cfreturn
      variables.instance.addressGW.filterAllAddresses(stuFilter) />
</cffunction>
```

Listing 7.12 – `AddressService.cfc` (Gateway method callers)

With the addition of the code in Listings 7.11 and 7.12 added to the basic structure for the `AddressService.cfc`, your service layer for the address packages is complete.

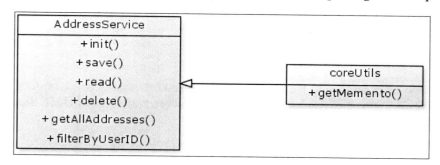

onApplicationStart (revisited)

Now that we have written our service layer objects, which interact with the DAO and Gateway for each package on our behalf, we can now amend the `onApplicationStart()` method within the `Application.cfc` file to build our objects.

From the four objects we were creating at the beginning of this chapter, we have streamlined the process and are now instantiating just two objects within the `onApplicationStart()` method; the User and Address service layers respectively.

Not only do these files provide a cleaner, simpler API with which to deal with the underlying code, but this also streamlines the process in which we create the objects. The Gateway and DAO, for each package, are now created within the `init()` method of each service object.

```
<cffunction name="onApplicationStart" output="false">

  <!--- Instantiate the Datasource object. --->
    <cfset var objDatasource = createObject('component',
      'com.packtApp.oop.beans.Datasource').init(
      DSName='CFOOP', username='< your datasource username >',
      password='< your datasource password >') />

  <!--- Instantiate and persist the User Service in the
      application scope.--->
    <cfset Application.userSVC = createObject('component',
      'com.packtApp.oop.dataAccess.UserService').init(
      datasource = objDatasource) />

  <!--- Instantiate and persist the Address Service in the
      application scope.--->
    <cfset Application.addressSVC = createObject('component',
      'com.packtApp.oop.dataAccess.AddressService').init(
      datasource = objDatasource) />
</cffunction>
```

Listing 7.13 - `Application.cfc` (after services)

Now that we have amended the `Application.cfc` component to instantiate the two Service objects instead of the four data-related objects, our revised UML diagram would look a little like this:

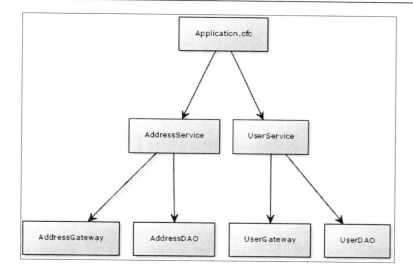

As we can see from the diagram, the `Application.cfc` merely needs to instantiate the service layers/facade objects, which in turn will create the required objects to access the underlying information from the data providers.

Summary

A Service Layer is responsible for providing simple and elegant access to application-specific business logic, data access functions, and methods contained in the Data Access Objects and Gateways, and can be used for creating the package Beans.

By calling these sometimes large, complicated methods through the facade pattern of the Service Layer, a simplified interface to the larger underlying code base is made available, providing quick, clean access to the 'important' functions that are required for application development.

This method of application architecture, however basic, will help to reduce the amount of time required to further enhance your application, and will help to ensure that any business-critical logic or SQL statements are kept safe and away from view, only being accessed by the Service Layer and its methods.

Other topics we have covered in this chapter are:

- streamlining the API
- extending a base class
- further code inheritance

Index

A

access attribute
about 46
package access option 47
private access option 46
public access option 47
remote option 47
accessors 67, 68
accessors attribute 82, 83
address service
defining 163-165
onApplicationStart() method, using 166, 167
revised UML diagram 166
aggregation
about 103
example 103-105
simple Driver object, creating 105-107
API 136
Application Programming Interface. *See* API
arguments
cfargument, using for method combination 27-29
functions, merging 26, 27
passing, into instance method call 25
arguments, passing into instance method call
as argumentCollection 26
as list 25
as named values 26

B

baseNumber() function 19
baseNumber() method 22, 47
Bean
about 59-62
benefits 62, 63
comparing, with ColdFusion component 66
creating 63
default/no-argument constructor 66
entity structure, populating 61
introspection, easy access 67
populating 73
projects Bean, calling 72, 73
projects Bean, completing 68-71
Bean, creating
UML 63
Bean, populating 74
Read-only Bean 76, 77
Read/Write Beans 74, 75

C

CFC
accessing 22
advantages 8
benefit 57
code documentation 50
component 7
component, creating 10
components, organizing 9, 10
functions, grouping 9
introspection 48

loading 9
metadata, obtaining 52
methods 7
need for 8
structure 7, 8
tags 10
uses 8
CFC, accessing
cfinvoke, using 23
object, instantiating 22
ways 22, 23
cffunction returnType attribute
any value 45
array value 45
boolean value 45
numeric value 45
query value 45
string value 45
struct value 45
void value 45
xml value 45
cfinvoke, CFC
argument collection, using 25
attributes, using as arguments 24, 25
cfinvokeargument, using 24
cfinvoke tag 24
using 23
class 10
code documentation
about 50
benefits 50
description attribute 51
displayname attribute 50
hint attribute 50, 51
user-defined metadata 51, 52
code duplication, minimizing
about 143
Gateway object, caching 147
gateway object, revising 144-146
ColdFusion
values, returning 42
variables, returning 42
ColdFusion Gateway
code duplication, minimizing 143
creating 136-138
methods, adding 140-142
naming conventions 138, 139

object, creating 138
qListUsers query 138
component, creating
data, ColdFusion 9 scripted components 12
data, returning 11
method, defining 11
object, creating 12
steps 10
composition
about 100
example 100
HAS A relationship 101-103
implied ownership 103
UML diagram 100
createNewuser() method
about 116-118
new user, storing 118-120
createObject() function 12, 22, 37
createObject() method 102
Create, Read, Update, and Delete. *See*
        CRUD
CRUD 112

D

DAO
about 111
caching 132
combining, with Table Gateway 150
creating 112
CRUD method 112
similarities, with Table Data Gateway 149
tasks 112
DAO, creating
about 112-116
createNewuser() method 116
delete method 128
exists() method 129
methods 113
read method 121
saveUser() method 129
update method 123
Data Access Object. *See* **DAO**
dateFormat() function 39
dateofbirth variable 78
delete() method 159
deleteUserByID() method 129

Dependency Injection. *See* DI
DI
  about 116, 133
  displaying 133

E

exists() method 130, 131

F

filterAllUsers() method 144
filterbyLastName() method 143
filterByParent() method 161
filterBy_X() method 158
filter_X() method 150
function restricting, to scope
  about 13
  Arguments scope 14
  argument, using 14
  function parameters, redefining 15, 16
  methods, combining 16, 17

G

Gateway
  about 135, 136, 148
  ColdFusion Gateway 136
  options, choosing 151
  Table Data Gateway 149
getAllUsers() function 149
getAll_x() method 150
getComponentMetaData() function 54, 55
getCurrentDate() method 38
getFullName() function 113
getID() method 131
getLastName() 78-80
getLastName() method 78-80
getMemento() function 162
getMemento() method 72
getMetaData() function 52
getMetaData() method 55
getName() function 14
getName() method 17, 100
getters 67, 68
getUserByID() method 121

H

HAS A relationship, composition
  about 101-103
  implied ownership 103
hasDriver() method 107

I

implicit accessors
  using, in Person.cfc 83, 84
inheritance
  about 87
  book, UML diagram 88
  code duplication, avoiding 90
  DVD object, UML diagram 89
  example 88
  hierarchy 98
  Product Base class, inheriting 93
  products, inheriting 91-95
  products, instantiating 96, 97
  super keyword, using 95
  UML diagram 91, 92
inheritance hierarchy
  about 98
  IS A relationship 99
  specialization 98, 99
init() method. *See* pseudo-constructor
introspection
  about 48
  CFC Explorer 48, 49
  Component Doc 49
Inversion of Control. *See* IoC
IoC 133

K

keyword
  super keyword 95
  Var keyword, using 20

L

local variables
  protecting 17-19
  Var scope, using 20, 21

M

metadata, CFC
 getComponentMetaData() function 54, 55
 getMetaData() function 52, 53
 obtaining 52
 returning 55, 56
method
 baseNumber() 22, 46
 createNewUser() 113
 createObject() 102
 deleteUser() 113
 deleteUserByID() 129
 exists() 130, 131
 filterAllUsers() 144
 filterbyLastName() 143
 filterByParent() 161
 getAllUsers() 140
 getCurrentDate() 38
 getMemento() 72
 getMetaData() function 55
 getName() 17, 100
 getUserByID() 113, 121
 hasDriver() 107
 nit() 37
 multiplyNumbers() 46
 onApplicationStart() 132, 166
 personalGreeting() 17
 saveUser() 129
 sayHello() 16
 updateUser() 113, 129
Model View Controller. *See* **MVC**
multiplyNumbers() function 19
multiplyNumbers() method 46
mutators 67
MVC 8

N

NEW operator 23

O

object constructor, creating
 about 29, 30
 init() function, calling 32
 init() function, creating 30, 31
 This scope 32-34

 Variables scope 31
object instantiation, CFC
 cfobject tag, using 23
 createObject function, using 22, 23
 methods 22
 NEW operator, using 23
object-oriented programming
 aggregation 103
 composition 100
 inheritance 87
 polymorphism 99
onApplicationStart() method 132, 147, 166
OOP design pattern. *See* **Bean**
output attribute 40

P

personalGreeting() function 26
personalGreeting() method 16, 17
Person.cfc UML diagram
 viewing 84
polymorphism
 about 99
 example 100
pseudo-constructor
 about 38
 output attribute 40, 41
 whitespace, suppressing 39
 using, in example 38, 39

Q

qListUsers, ColdFusion Gateway 138
query functions
 adding, into UserGateway Object 140-142

R

read method
 select results, handling 122, 123
read() method 159
returnType attribute
 using 42-44

S

save() method 159
saveUser() method 129, 130

sayHello() method 16
Service Layer
  about 154
  creating 155-157
  facade pattern 155
Service Layer, creating
  abstract class, adding 162
  User Service, defining 157
setters 67
sleepyStomachRumble() method 154
subclasses 90
super-component 90
super keyword, inheritance
  methods, overriding 95, 96
  using 95

T

Table Data Gateway
  about 149
  combining, with DAO 150
  similarities, with DAO 149
tags, CFC
  cfargument 10
  cfcomponent 10
  cffunction 10
  cfproperty 10

U

UDF 9
UML
  about 63
  person object 64
  structure 64, 66
Unified Modeling Language. *See* UML
updateUser() method 123-129
User-Defined Function. *See* UDF
User Service, defining
  about 157, 158
  CRUD methods, adding 158-160
  Gateway methods, adding 160, 161
  purpose 157

V

Var scope, using
  variables, naming 21, 22
  variables, placing 21

X

xml value, cffunction returnType attribute
  45

PUBLISHING

ColdFusion 9
Developer Tutorial

Create robust professional web applications
with ColdFusion

John Farrar   PACKT

ColdFusion 9 Developer Tutorial

ISBN: 978-1-849690-24-9   Paperback: 388 pages

Create robust professional web applications with
ColdFusion

1. Fast-paced guide to the foundational concepts
   of developing in ColdFusion

2. Broad coverage of CFScript to deal with its
   expanded power in ColdFusion 9

3. Enhance the user interface with built-in
   ColdFusion AJAX features (layout, forms, script,
   maps, and more)

4. Packed with example code and real-world
   knowledge

ColdFusion 8 Developer Tutorial

An intense guide to creating professional ColdFusion web
applications: get up to speed in ColdFusion and learn how to
integrate with other web 2.0 technologies

John Farrar   PACKT

ColdFusion 8 Developer Tutorial

ISBN: 978-1-847194-12-1   Paperback: 400 pages

An intense guide to creating professional ColdFusion
web applications: get up to speed in ColdFusion
and learn how to integrate with other web 2.0
technologies

1. Fast-paced guide to important ColdFusion
   development topics

2. Packed with example code and real-world
   knowledge

3. Coverage of using AJAX in ColdFusion

4. Also covers ColdFusion 8 Update 1

Please check **www.PacktPub.com** for information on our titles

Python 3 Object Oriented Programming

ISBN: 978-1-849511-26-1   Paperback: 404 pages

Harness the power of Python 3 objects

1. Learn how to do Object Oriented Programming in Python using this step-by-step tutorial

2. Design public interfaces using abstraction, encapsulation, and information hiding

3. Turn your designs into working software by studying the Python syntax

4. Raise, handle, define, and manipulate exceptions using special error objects

C# 2008 and 2005 Threaded Programming: Beginner's Guide

ISBN: 978-1-847197-10-8   Paperback: 416 pages

Exploit the power of multiple processors for faster, more responsive software

1. Develop applications that run several tasks simultaneously to achieve greater performance, scalability, and responsiveness in your applications

2. Build and run well-designed and scalable applications with C# parallel programming.

3. In-depth practical approach to help you become better and faster at managing different processes and threads

Please check **www.PacktPub.com** for information on our titles

LaVergne, TN USA
22 October 2010
201858LV00003B/12/P